Ra

Rats as pets
Rat Keeping, Pros and Cons, Care, Housing, Diet and
Health.
by

Roger Rodendale

Table of Contents

Introduction

A rat may seem like the most unusual choice for a pet. But these creatures are highly intelligent with a brain structure that, scientists believe, is very close to that of a human being.

The domesticated rat is also called a fancy rat. The hobby of having rats as pets originated several years ago and continues to enthrall several individuals.

If you are a young family looking for the ideal pet, then the low maintenance rat is your perfect choice. These animals are friendly, furry and quite intelligent as well.

Domesticated rats are quite different from the wild relative and have been bred for years to be the ideal house pet. The biggest and most important reason for the pet rat to gain popularity is that the domestic varieties do not pose any threat with respect to diseases. They can be harmful only when exposed to wild rats. If not, they do not necessarily carry any pathogens.

These rats do most of the work for you as they care for themselves for the most part. In comparison to the other smaller pets like hamsters, these animals are a lot more affordable. This is one of the prime reasons why people are drawn to them.

These creatures are highly independent, can be trained very easily and are certainly less work in comparison to other common pets like dogs and cats. There are several varieties of these domesticated rats. They are also considered to be the most intelligent among other rodents that are chosen to be house pets.

While they are more economic and do most of the care taking themselves, it does not mean that they are not a big responsibility. Once you have a rat in your home, you need to keep him healthy and clean. They should be free from any diseases as some of them are zoonotic, which means that they are passed on to human beings.

A rat is definitely a unique choice for a pet. This also means that you will not be able to find too many rat owners who can help you with common issues and queries. This is why you need to gather as much information as you can about feeding, housing and caring for your potential rat pet.

This book covers everything that you need to know about having a rat as a pet. It also discusses in detail the advantages and disadvantages of having a rat as a pet.

The idea is to educate novices in the world of rats and provide assistance to those who already have some experience with these rodents as pets. All the information in this book is a compilation of practical tips that you can use as a rat parent.

It tells you everything from where you can buy your rodent to how you should deal with issues like breeding or healthcare. The goal is to make sure that everyone makes an informed decision when bringing a rat home so that the family and the pet can live a good life.

Chapter 1: Know the Fancy Rat

The domestic rat or fancy rat, as it is popularly called, is quite an interesting animal. Being markedly different from the wild rat, this breed also has dedicated clubs and societies that decide the standards for the physical appearance.

One of the most well-known organizations is the American Fancy Rat and Mouse Association. This was founded in the year 1983 as an international, non-profit club.

The goal of the organization is to promote the interest in fancy mice and rats and to also educated people about providing proper care to their pets. There are also several shows and competitions that are organized by this organization to create more interest in exhibiting companion rats.

Most of these shows are held in Southern California. They also have classes for these companion rats and mice to prepare them for shows and to teach owners how to take good care of them. One of the simplest ways to stay updated about pet rat care is to sign up for a membership with this club or any other fancy rat club in your country or state.

You will have the advantage of frequent newsletters and pamphlets that will give you medical information, pet care information, showing information and also other informative material.

Some of the other clubs that are working towards better care for pet mice and rats are the National Fancy Rat Society, the Australian Rat Fanciers Society, the German Rat Fancy Society, Ratoonga in South Africa, The North of England Rat Society and the Canadian Pet Rat Club.

According to these societies and clubs, a pet rat must possess certain qualities that ensure that they are in good health. The next section tells you in detail about the proper physical appearance of domesticated rats.

1. General description

The general appearance of the rat should be pleasant. They should have a good outline and must seem to be alert and attentive. The body of a fancy rat is long and the posture should make the animal look lively, almost like he is bred for racing. The bone structure should be smooth and strong. The loin region on the body should have a visible arch.

The one quality that you should look for when you are buying a pet rat is that the body should be of good weight. The rat must not look too skinny or plump. A rat who is of the ideal weight will show emphasized physical qualities.

The coat of the animal is short, glossy and smooth in most varieties. The hair on the males is coarser and longer. A well maintained rat will have a natural shine in the coat. In addition to that, the body must be densely covered with fur.

As for the head, it must have a clean outline and must be long. The muzzle should not be too fine or pointed. You must be able to see good breadth as well as length in the skull. The distance between the ears and the eyes shouldn't be too little or too large. The whiskers are also a sign of good health. They will usually appear straight and long, except in the case of some varieties like the satin and the hairless rats.

The most noticeable feature in fancy rats is the eyes. They must be prominent, bold and large. They should look lively and must also be animated.

The shape of the ears is also an important standard with rats. The ears should be erect and must not have any creases or folds. They should be set far apart and must be rounded and of good size.

The tail of the fancy rat is thick at the base and comes out of the back distinctly. It will taper to a small point in the end and must not have any kinks. The length of the tail is usually equal to the length of the body. A tail that is longer than the body is acceptable while one that is shorter is usually not accepted according to the standards set by these associations.

While size does not really come under a judging standard or a general standard of appearance in the case of rats, the larger the rat, the better. On average, when measured from the nose to the tip of the tail, the rat measures about 10 inches. Males are slightly larger in size when compared to the females.

In general, rats should be easy to handle and tractable or docile. If you notice any unsteadiness in temperament or see any noticeable physical defects, it is best that you do not choose that rat as a pet. They can be challenging pets in such cases.

In addition to that, if you wish to show your rats, the judging criteria requires them to adhere to all the standards set. They must also be of good temperament without which they can be eliminated from these shows.

In the following sections, we will learn about the defects and faults that you need to keep in mind when choosing your pet rat. You will also get all the information you need about the temperament of the rat and what to expect from him.

2. Types of rats

Over the years, people have taken to breeding fancy rats as a serious hobby. Some qualities like markings and colorations have been pursued and new ones have been developed over a period of time. Today there are several varieties of fancy rats to choose from. They as classified based on the coloration, the markings and there also are some standard varieties that are more common than the other. Here are the different varieties of fancy rats that are available:

Standard varieties
These are the most common types of fancy rats and are also known as "Self varieties".

Pink Eye: These rats are pure white in color all over the body with no markings or any tinge of cream or any stains. They have brilliant pink eyes which gives them the name.

Champagne: They have a slight beige or champagne colored tinge on the body. The eyes are red in color.

Buff: The body is an even and warm magnolia tone without any grey coloration or dullness in the color. The color of the eye is a dark ruby shade.

Platinum: The body has a pale grey coloration with hue of ice blue. These rats have no strong tones of blue or any brownish or creamy coloration. The color of the eye ranges from red to ruby.

Quick Silver: These rats have a grey coat without any tinge of blue. The under color may have a shade of light blue or can be skin colored. The color of the feet is also grey while the eyes are either pale or dark ruby colored.

British Blue: The coat has a distinct steel blue coloration without any tinge of brown. The coloration is maintained at blue grey till the skin and can be seen when you part the fur.

Black: These rats have a solid black coat without any patches or strands of white. The feet and the eyes are also black in color.

Chocolate: The fur has a rich chocolate coloration. There must not be any patches or strands of white hair. The eyes are black in color while the feet match the color of the fur.

Mink: They have a grey brown coat that is mid-toned. Silver strands and patches should not be present. They should also not have a bluish tinge to the fur. The color of the foot matches the fur and the eyes are usually black in color.

Ivory: The color of the body is creamy white and pale. There are no odd patches or strands of hair. The tail is pink in color while the eyes are black.

Varieties depending on marking

The mutations that have occurred over the years have given rise to several interesting markings on the fur. The most common varieties based on coloration are:

Berkshire: The body is marked symmetrically with a lot of white markings on the belly and the chest. These colorations should not extend to the sides of the body and have clear cuts with no traces of brindling. The back feet are white up to the ankle while half the front legs are white. The tail is white for half the length. The color of the body depends on the variety of the animal. Some of these Berkshire rats may have a white spot on the forehead along with symmetrical suspenders.

Badger: The underside of the rat is white for the most part including the throat, the belly, chest and the feet without this coloration going up the sides. The limbs are white until the joints. Half the length of the tail is white in color. A very marked quality with this variety is the blaze of white fur that starts at the nose and extends up to the forehead. It is wedge shaped and covers the whisker bed without extending to the eyes or the cheeks.

Irish: An equilateral triangular marking on the neck is the trademark of the Irish variety. The front and back feet are white for half the length. The triangular marking needs to be clear and should not have any brindling. It also does not extend to the belly and should stop in the space between the front legs.

Hooded: There is a distinct hood like marking that covers the head, the chest and shoulders. In the lighter color varieties there may be pale colored skin on the chest and the throat. The hood is continuous and runs down the spine and extends till the tail. The width of this saddle is between 1-2 cms. The hood has a clear edge and does not have any brindling. The rest of the body is usually white in color.

Variegated: The head and the shoulders are of the same distinct color. There is a white blaze or spot on the forehead. The spot, when present, is in the center of the forehead and is the same size as the eye of the rat. The blaze is wedge shaped and symmetrical. It is just over the nose and extends all the way to the forehead. This blaze covers the whole whisker bed and tapers into a fine spot in between the eyes. The upper portion of the body is white and marked evenly with flecks and patches that are of a distinct color. The underside is usually white without any staining or tinge.

Capped: The color of the head is different from the body. This unique coloration does not go past the ears and is along the lower jay. There is a spot or white blaze on the forehead while the rest of the body is also white.

Essex: The top color is lightened. The darkest part of the fur runs along the spine and becomes lighter around the sides. This fading continues and leads to a white belly. The light and dark fur should blend in and not be demarcated. The feet are white with the same fading effect on the legs. Patches of contrasting colors are not acceptable with this variety. The head has a white spot or blaze that is placed in the center and is symmetrical.

Chinchilla: This variety has a top grey color with strands of black and a white ground color. This makes the rat have a sparkling appearance. The undercolor is usually dark slate blue. There may be head markings in some cases. A spot or blaze is also noticed in some cases. The forelegs are white for half their length. The tail is pied.

Squirrel: The top color is silver blue which is the result of blue guard hair interspersed with pearl white ground hair. The under color is a distinct slate blue while the underside is white in color. A blaze or spot can be seen on the head. The forelegs are white for half the length while the hind legs are white till the hocks. The tail is usually pied.

Roan: This is a bi colored variety that is symmetrical and yet contrasting in colors. This distinguishes them from the other marked varieties of rats. They are solid colored at birth and the roan effect is seen at about 4-6 weeks of age. The underside is fully white. The head has an inverted v-shaped blaze. The jawline and the underside of the head are also white in color. The tail is usually unmarked. When the contrast of the marking is high, the variety is usually known as the striped roan as the two colors of the fur as distinctly different from one another and not just a lighter shade.

Other varieties
The other types of coloration or varieties found are:

Cream: The color of the body is a warm or clotted shade of cream. There are no odd colors or other patches that are seen. The belly is a pale cream color. The ears and the tail are pink while the eyes can either be black or pink.

Topaz: These rats are golden fawn in color with some silver guard hair. The under color is either grey or pale blue and is carried to the skin. The belly fur is cream silver in color. The eyes are dark ruby in color.

Silver fawn: These rats have a rich orange fawn coating with intermingling silver guard hair. The belly fur is pure white in color. The eyes are red.

Silver: They have a coat that is half silver and half black, mink, British blue or chocolate. The silver strands may have colored tips. This silver fur gives the coat a sparkling appearance. The color of the foot matches the other color besides silver. The belly is either cinnamon or silver. In some cases, the belly fur matches the color of the top.

Agouti: The fur is a rich ruddy brown color. The guard hairs are black in color. The base is dark grey or black in color. The color of the foot must match the color of the top. The eyes are distinctly black in color.

Cinnamon: The color of the fur is a warm tone of brown. They also have ticks of chocolate colored guard hairs. The belly fur is the same as the agouti variety but slightly lighter. The eyes are black in color.

British Blue Agouti: These are among the most attractive rats with a fawn ground color and mid-blue ticks. The belly color is silver. The feet are grey and the ears and tail are covered with blue fur. The eyes are black.

Lilac agouti: The ground is medium fawn in color with ticks of dove grey hairs. The under color is a pale grey that goes down to the skin. The belly fur is silver. The ears and the tail are covered in grey hair. They may also have a pinkish tinge. The eyes are either black or dark ruby red.

Pearl: These rats are of the palest shade of silver. The under color is cream. Every strand of hair has a grey tip. The belly fur is creamy silver in color. The foot matches the top color. The eyes are black.

Cinnamon pearl: These rats have three color bands from the base which are cream, blue and orange. They have silver guard hairs to make the rat look almost golden. The belly fur is pale grey in color. The foot matches the top. The eyes are black in color.

Rex: These rats have a coat that is curled evenly to give it a rough look and this curling reduces towards the belly. These rats may also have curled whiskers. They can be of any color, with any marking.

Dumbo: The ears are the distinct characteristic of these rats. They are set low, on the sides of the head. The base is at the back of the cheek and the ears are much wider than the standard rat. The ears stand at a prominent angle and have a shape that resembles a rose petal. The head is shaped like any standard rat although it looks different because of the ears. The back of the skull has a prominent hunchback appearance.

Knowing about each variety in detail will make it a lot easier for you to choose a furry buddy when you decide to bring one home.

3. Origin of domesticated rats

The lives of human beings and rats have been connected ever since human beings began to farm and stopped being hunter-gatherers. As humans learnt how to grow and store grains, rats found an easy food source. Rats also sought shelter in human dwellings and began to stay safer and grow in population.

Although this relationship was not amiable, it was not long before someone decided to catch one of these pests and raise it as their own. The first ever pet rat is believed to be an Agouti colored wild rat. There were several different mutations even among the wild rats and when people found one that was very unusually colored, they would often catch them and keep them as pets and also interesting oddities.

The rats that we know as fancy rats today originated from the Norway rat or the brown rat. These rats had large colonies in Europe, especially England around the 18th century. These brown rats were larger and were able to adapt better. They were able to live in environments that were not suitable for the regular black rat and soon outnumbered them. During this time the whole of England became outrun with rats, both black and white.

Capturing rats in rat pits

With the increase in the rat population, an interesting sport emerged. This sport led to a lot of rats being captured in Victorian England to be used in the rat pits. This became a popular pastime in London. Several rats were confined in a small enclosure with a dog. The dog would then begin to hunt down these rats and the one that was able to kill the most in the shortest period of time became the winner. Bets were placed on these dogs. As a result, the establishments exchanged large amounts of money.

It was common for mutations to occur and every once in a while, a rat with unusual coloration would end up in these pits. And, most owners kept and bred these oddly colored rats. Jimmy Shaw who managed one of the most well-known and largest public sporting houses bred rats that were strangely colored. It was even possible that he sold them to others as pets.

Jack Black- The Royal Rat Catcher

The problem with wild rats was that they were increasing in population in England and some measure had to be taken to control their population. This task was assigned to Jack Black who was the Royal Rat Catcher. He is, to this day, credited for breeding the first true fancy rat or domesticated rat.

As he caught these wild rats, he kept the ones that were unusually colored and bred them. He had a collection of Fawn, Grey, Albino, Black and even Marked specimens that he bred to sell as pets. It was between the 1840s and the 1860s that he and Jimmy Shaw sold the most number of rats. This is believed to be the origin of the modern fancy rat.

The First Ever Fancy Rat

In the early 1800s, Europe developed a fancy for colored mice, especially the UK. It was then in 1895 that the National Mouse Club of England was formed. This club set all the standards for the various types of mice to enter them in shows. With this club, the fancy rat also came into being.

Miss Mary Douglas who is also known as the "mother of rat fancy" approached the club in 1901 and asked them to also include rats. The club agreed to this and staged several classes of domesticated rats in fall the same year. In less than two years, the interest in rats grew so much that the name of the organization was changed to National Mouse and Rat Club.

During this time, one of the biggest subjects of discussion in the scientific community was Mendel's genetic theory. Fancy rats were the best models to conduct more research. They were easy to house because of their size, they were inexpensive and they also reproduced rather quickly. This is when they gained popularity in the field of research for several subjects.

After the death of Miss Douglas in the year 1921, the popularity of the fancy rat also began to decline. For the next few years, people would show less interest in rats. They became so unpopular that in 1929, the word rat was dropped from the name of the club. Even to this day, the National Mouse Club functions and assists those with interests in mice.

The birth of the NFRS

For the next 45 years, people showed sporadic interest in fancy rats. There were several considerations for a rat club but all of them never took off because of a lack of support. Finally in January 1976, the National Fancy Rat Society was formed. This club was the first one that was dedicated exclusively to rats. They published newsletters, set standards and even held shows. Since then, fancy rats grew in popularity quite enormously. Ever since, several varieties have been introduced and standardized.

There is no clear understanding of the interest in rats in the United States. It is possible that people occasionally caught a wild rat and kept it with them as a pet. However, no written records are available to document these instances.

Most of the fancy rats in the United States were kept in science labs. Pet care books that were written as early as the 1920s show records of people contacting universities or local labs in order to obtain white rats. When they were unable to get one from these sources, they contacted animal suppliers or pet stores. Most people who bred rats for these pet stores also supplied them to the pet stores.

Rat fancy in the United States

Rat fancy in the USA became popular only recently. The first ever club in the USA was the Mouse and Rat Breeders Association. This club was formed in the year 1978. Then, in the year 1983, the American Fancy Rat and Mouse Association came into being.

After the formation of these clubs, several rats were imported from England. Today, these imports have made it possible to obtain all the varieties of these fancy rats in the USA as well.

There are also several fanciers in the USA who have bred rats to create their own varieties. Today, there are several clubs in the USA as well as all across the globe that are dedicated especially to fancy rats.

A boom in the interest towards fancy rats was seen over the last 15 years. They have gained a lot of importance not only as pets but also as show animals. The current population of reptiles in the domesticated set up has also increased because of the increased rat population in the USA. People were able to buy these rats easily to feed their reptiles. In the process, they also discovered that rats make wonderful pets.

Today, people long for the companionship of a furry friend. However, they do not have the time, the money or the space for these pets. The fancy rat is the perfect alternative. They are great pocket pets and are also highly receptive and intelligent.

This is a trend that will only grow in popularity. If you are also an ardent rat fancier, the next section will talk about the ten reasons why these rats make the ideal pet. We also discuss the flipside to make sure that you know what you are getting into.

Ten reasons why they make the best pets
Rats have a reputation of being pests and are hence the most underrated household pets. They can become your best pal if you are willing to give them a chance. These animals are accustomed to being around people and can be just as adorable as any other rodent that is commonly kept as a pet such as the hamster or the guinea pig.

In fact, they can make even better pets than them. Here are 10 reasons why rats make the best pets and companions:

1. **They have a great personality:** The best thing about a rat is that each one has a different personality than the other. This is something that people do not generally expect from small pets. They can be mischievous and extremely outgoing. They also have varying intelligence levels and abilities to learn. Some of them are extremely smart while others need some coaxing to be trained.

   As rats grow up, they also form strong bonds with their owners. The personality develops as per you interaction with the rat.

2. **They are very low maintenance pets:** If there is some situation such as too much work or any other kind of stress that does not let you spend too much time with rats, they are not as negatively impacted as other pets. They are extremely hardy and will be able to keep themselves entertained with the toys or with their cage mates. That said, you cannot neglect your pet but, at the same time, you can take on responsibilities without the fear of making your pet feel neglected. As long as it is not a long term separation, your pet rat will be fine.

3. **They are extremely loving and will form close bonds:** Unlike popular belief, rats can be very affectionate and family oriented. They live in groups, also known as mischiefs, that are very close knit and will spend a lot of time either grooming or playing with each other. These animals like your attention. If you cannot give your pet rat any attention, then you can get him a cage mate and watch them play and create a riot!

4. **They are very clean:** Rats are generally associated with dirty places or the garbage. However, as pets, they can be extremely clean. Their cages have designated areas to relieve themselves and the rats will not dirty any other area. If course, they do have a sense of territory which makes them leave a little bit of their urine on their belongings to leave some scent. It is also possible to potty train these animals to use a litter box.

5. **They are very economical:** As far as the basic needs are concerned, rats are very cheap. Their food is cheap and you can use several things from your home to make toys for them. Most of the food that we eat such as fruits, grains, vegetables and meat can be given to them. That means that you only have to take a small portion of your cooking out for your rat.

6. **They are highly trainable:** It is possible to train rats to understand a host of commands. They have the ability to distinguish between rewards and punishment and are quick to associate the behavior with them. They are even believed to be able to pick up verbal commands. For instance, they can learn their names and are also able to understand what is happening around them. In fact, these creatures can be taught some complex tasks. In some countries, rats are used to rewire areas that humans are unable to get into, work as messengers and even detect landmines.

7. **They are extremely friendly:** In comparison to other pets, rats are less likely to develop aggressive behavior. This is one of the reasons why they are recommended as pets for younger children. If your rat is healthy and is bought from a good breeder, they are very well behaved. Rats that have been bred properly and almost never bite. Even when they are brought home from a rescue shelter or from an inexperienced breeder, they tend to be very docile. They do not bite unless they feel threatened or are experiencing some sort of health issue.

8. **They are very healthy:** If you take good care of a rat from birth, he will stay very healthy. They rarely fall sick and are immune to most diseases. The only major health concern is with females who tend to develop mammary cancer. If the rat is spayed or has been mated to give birth to a litter at least once after becoming sexually mature, this risk also reduces. Besides that, you need to make sure that you give the rat good food, ample space and a good amount of exercise to keep them healthy.

9. **They are easy to find:** For those who want to bring home a rat, they are relatively easier to find. There are several ratteries and professional breeders from where you can source your rat. In addition to that, they can be found with hobby breeders and also in pet shops. Another option is to adopt one from a shelter.

10. **There are several varieties:** Rats are available in several shapes and colors. There are also different sizes of rats that you can choose as per your requirement. The best part is that any type of rat that you choose is invariably adorable and extremely cute. As we discussed before, there are Dumbo rats, rex rats and even ones that are hairless or tailless. Since they are so easy to breed, several new varieties are introduced almost every day. Each one is more stunning than the last.

Rats are, no doubt, excellent companions. But, all you need to do is invest some time and effort to build a good relationship with your rat and they become a part of the family. Besides that, you need to understand that though they are extremely low maintenance, they are a responsibility from the time you bring them home.

4. Difference between wild and domesticated rats

If you are having trouble convincing your family about bringing home a rat as a pet, then it would help for them to know that the domesticated rat is quite different from the wild one.

Since most people associate rats with pests, it does seem like the rat is a very unlikely pet to have. The negative association is because rats have carried deadly diseases like bubonic plague that resulted in the death of many people in the 17th century.

However, with fancy rats catching the eye of hobby rats, domesticated rats have become popular pets. So, to make it simpler to make your whole family fall in love with your potential pet, here are a few differences between the domesticated rat and wild rats:

Social behavior

In the wild, rats are known to be very unsocial. They will flee at the sight of human beings and will try their best to escape. In case they do not find any place to escape, they often become hostile and may even attack the person. Domestic rats on the other hand are quite friendly and social towards human beings. The instances of domesticated rats biting humans are very few and normally occur when the rats feel extremely threatened.

Size

Normally, rats grow to a size of 11 to 12 inches. However, in the wild, rats are unable to reach their full size because they do not live long enough. The maximum size that they grow to is about 10 inches. These rats are also thinner in comparison to domesticated ones because they do not get as much food. The only time these rats appear large is when they puff their fur up to look large to predators. In comparison to wild rats, domesticated rats are heavier while the former are leaner. The most common cause of this bulkiness in domesticated rats is the fact that they do not receive as much exercise as they need.

Domestic rats have a larger lifespan and will therefore attain the full size of 11-12 inches.

Coloration

Domesticated rats have varied colors. They come in several colors like beige, grey, tan and black. There are several other varieties of domesticated rats, which is the result of interbreeding. One of the most popular types of domesticated rats is the white rat which is pink eyed. This rat has been common since the beginning of the 19th century. In the case of wild rats, they are usually brown or black in color. In case of the brown ones, the under belly is white or light brown.

Adaptation

When it comes to adapting to any captive environment, wild rats are not entirely comfortable as they do not have any place to hide in. These rats need dark spaces and are usually bothered by bright light. When held in captivity, wild rats usually succumb to the stress or will not be able to reproduce. Even when they mate and have a litter, the baby rats will be much smaller than expected for the first generation. It takes 20 generations for the babies of wild rats to develop normally. Similarly, when a domesticated rat is introduced into the wild, they are seldom able to survive and adapt. They do not have the behavioral skills and the physical make-up to survive. They may survive in the wild if the environment is controlled by humans.

So you see, there is a vast difference between wild and domesticated rats. If you are sure that you want to bring home a pet rat, the first thing that you need to do is pick a healthy one for your home and introduce him to your environment.

Chapter 2: Buying a Pet Rat

Buying a fancy rat requires some research and understanding of the different sources available to you. Since the interest in these domesticated rats spiked, there have been several hobby breeders and commercial breeders who have worked towards creating new varieties of fancy rats.

However, not all these sources will help you buy a healthy pet for your home. Some of them engage in unethical practices that will leave you with an unhealthy pet. This chapter tells you all that you need to know about buying a fancy rat.

1. Finding a good breeder

One of the best ways to buy a rat is directly from a breeder. This will help you learn about the history of the animal and also the conditions that they have been raised in. You can also check the health and medical history of the parents to prevent any unexpected issues.

There are several clubs that maintain a register of breeders who are often members of these clubs. This is the best way to look for a breeder in your locality or in your town. These breeders advertise regularly on the official websites of these clubs allowing you to find the exact variety that you are looking for.

Whether you are looking for a fancy rat for breeding, showing or just to be your companion for life, you can look for a breeder who will match your specific requirements. You can even ask around with people who already have pet rats for recommendations.

The key to finding a healthy pet is to look for breeders who adhere to the guidelines set by prominent clubs like the National Fancy Rat Society or the American fancy Rat and Mouse Association. Before you pick a breeder, here are a few questions you can ask them to ensure that you are dealing with a genuine one.

Do they deal in feeder rats?

If the breeder that you approach sells feeder rats, then it is a big red flag. These breeders are usually not very concerned about the health of the baby rats. Feeder rats are those rats that are bred only to be fed to reptiles, such as snakes, as food.

When you see an advertisement that suits your requirements, call the breeder and ask for feeder rats. They are usually bought in groups of 4-5. You can even claim to be willing to pay a premium cost. If the breeder agrees, then you need to look elsewhere. This is a clear sign that the rats are being raised purely for profit and can mean that you will end up with a rat with behavioral issues like biting.

What kind of cages are used by the breeder?

This is one of the most important things to ask the breeder. The cages affect the health and the behavior of the rat to a large extent. It is mandatory for the rats to have enough space. The male and the female units should have enough space between them. Rat racks should not be used in the cage and not more than three rats must be bred in a cage at one time. The cages should also have enough ventilation.

Most commercial breeders use an aquarium as it is the simplest and the cheapest option available. One can find aquariums for less than $20. However, these aquariums do not allow air flow and put the health of the rats at risk. The flooring should not have wires or ramps. They cause severe damage to the feet and can lead to severe health issues like bumble foot.

Do they use rat racks?

Rat racks are the worst housing option for rats. In most cases the rat racks are not used properly either. These rat racks are cages with multiple units that are usually made of about 8 tubs and trays. They are about 5-10 gallons in size and are usually made from a large aquarium. In most models, there is no room for any light in the cage. The bedding used in these rat racks is usually cedar or pine, which make the rats very unwell. You can ask the breeder to show you the setup used for the rats if you have any concerns.

Are you being shown underweight or sick animals?

Sometimes breeders will offer unwell animals for free just to get rid of them. If you are an experienced rat owner, then you may opt to rescue these animals from their misery. You can even bring them with you to a rescue shelter. However, if the breeder quotes a price for these rats, refuse to pay for them. Any funds given to these breeders is as good as sponsoring an unethical practice. Instead, choose to inform any rescue shelter or animal rights authority about the plight of the animals at the breeder.

What are the rats being fed?

There are several options available when it comes to feeding rats. There are some highly recommended formulae such as Oxbow. Some breeders may also choose to make healthy home mixes for their animals. However, if the breeder is providing only rat seed mix, hamster mix, bird seed or dog food to the rats, then it is a sign of poor breeding. These animals are usually undernourished and will have several health issues associated with poor feeding.

What bedding is the breeder using?

You have several bedding options for rats. But there are some that need to be completely avoided, such as cedar or any type of wood. Some types of wood such as Aspen are often acceptable. Most of these wood based bedding material contain toxins that can even kill the rats.

Breeders choose wood bedding because it is the cheapest option available. Some of them use newspapers that are also harmful because of the toxins present in the ink. Wood or newspaper is a sign of a less concerned breeder.

Some preferred bedding options for rats are recycled paper or fleece liners. These are healthy and safe. Of course, they are a tad bit more expensive. If the breeder is willing to make the investment, then it means that he genuinely cares about the health and well-being of the animals.

Does the breeder have any negative reviews online?

Today, the Internet is the best way to source any information that you need. The first thing that you can do is Google the name of the breeder or the name of the rattery. You will possibly find several advertisements, websites and even social medial pages. The next thing to do is to look for reviews on these sources. You can gather a lot of information about the breeder through the Internet.

There may be some negative reviews even for the most recommended breeders. If you find just one or two bad reviews among several good ones, then you do not have to be very concerned. However, 3 reviews or more, especially when they are several months apart, can be a red flag.

Does the breeder only show interest in the profits earned from sales?

There are several commercial breeders who are all about the profits. You will understand what the priority of the breeder is with a simple conversation. If most of the conversation is about the price and less about the health of the animal or tips about caring, then chances are that you have approached a feeder breeder. In most cases, hobby breeders and breeders who are passionate about raising rats will usually price them in a way that allows them to fund the care for the rats in their rattery.

Is the breeder able to answer simple questions about caring for pet rats?

Doing some homework and learning the basics of rat care will help you test the breeder that you approach. You can then ask them a few simple questions about raising rats. If you feel that they have more misses with these questions than hits, then it speaks for their experience and interest in caring for the rats. It is recommended to look for a different breeder even if you find one unsatisfactory answer. Here are some questions that you can ask the breeder that you approach:

- What are the best bedding options for rats?
- What can I feed my pet rat?
- How early should the litter mates be separated?
- Can I use an aquarium?
- How do I pick the rat up safely?

Are the health records of the animals available?

All good breeders make sure that they have the health record of their animals in place. They should at least be able to tell you what illnesses have been seen among the animals. In some cases, the breeder may be lucky with no health issues with his animals although this is very unlikely. Many breeders, even the good ones, have seen cases of mites, blindness, myco flares, mammary tumors and others. This is a part of breeding rats. They are prone to certain health issues even after cautious care.

Make sure you ask about the parents of the rat that you plan to buy. This will give you a good idea about what to expect in terms of the genetics of the rat. If you are looking at breeding your rats, then this information is very valuable. Even if your pets have an accidental litter, knowing about the health history and the genetics will keep you prepared.

When you buy from breeders who are not entirely concerned about the health of the animals, then you are could be signing up for a nightmare. Rats that are unhealthy can become defensive and easily threatened. This leads to issues like biting and even severe aggression in some cases.

This is why choosing the right breeder is the most important step towards having a pet rat that can become a great companion.

Common guidelines for breeders
When you are aware of the most common guidelines for rat breeders, you will be able to tell if the one you have approached is adhering to them or not. Here are some guidelines that are common to most countries. The guidelines ensure prevention of any malpractice and sale of only healthy and eligible animals:

- The rat that is being sold should be healthy.

- Any rat that is under six weeks of age or over 3 months of age should not be sold.

- Pregnant rats must not be sold unless there is a prior agreement between the breeder and the buyer. If a breeder sells you a pregnant rat unwittingly or on purpose, the onus of caring for the baby rats is entirely upon you.

- When a rat is sold to you, all the details such as the date of birth, the name of the seller and contact details should be provided. This will help you deal with any complaints or enquiries easily.

- If a breeder makes unfounded claims about the rat that he is selling to you, then it is against the Sales of Goods Act 1979. Some breeders will tell you, for instance, that the rat is show winning. Unless the rat or his parents have actually won a show, this is an offence.

- The Supply of Goods Act 1973, makes it a criminal offence to display any disclaimer or exclusion. The breeder should be willing to take the sold rat back if there is any complain within a fortnight of the sale. If you are bringing home a pregnant rat, then this period is extended to twenty three days. In case of any issue in this regard, you can approach the executive committee of a rat club in your city or state.

- Rats must never be sold to children under the age of 16 unless they are accompanied by an adult, mandatorily the parent or the guardian.

- All states and the concerned clubs set a minimum price for the rats. They should not be sold below this price. Currently, this minimum price is $5 or £7.

- The male and female kittens should be separated within 4-5 weeks of birth to avoid mating and accidental litters.

- The breeder should not isolate the rats, as they are social animals. It is advisable to keep rats in groups of 2 or more. These groups should include pairs or same sex individuals to ensure better health and physical condition.

- The breeder should give you all his contact details. This will help solve any problems and will also allow you to deal with any complaints without any hassle. It is also mandatory in some cases for the breeder to also provide a family tree of the rats.

- The parent rats chosen for each breeding cycle should be healthy. If the breeder is using rats that are not sound physically or rats that have an uneven temperament for breeding purposes, chances are that the offspring will gave the same issues.

- The breeder should not choose animals that are too young or old for mating. For instance the doe or the female should be between 5 to 7 months of age. If the doe is older than one year of age, she may encounter several problems with respect to her pregnancy.

- Kittens usually cost between $5-$15 or £7-£20 and the cost may vary as per the breeder and the variety of the rat.

- Breeders reserve as much right to check if you are suitable owners. In fact, a breeder who is concerned about the home that their rats will go into are genuinely interested in the well-being of their rats. They can ask you several questions about your lifestyle and also your background before selling a rat to you. If the breeder is not convinced that you will take good care of the rats, he reserves every right to refuse a sale to you.

- The breeder can also use an application form to learn about your background and intention with the rats.

Genuine breeders expect potential owners to have some information about housing, handling and caring for rats. This is a reasonable expectation from any potential pet parent.

When you make some effort in learning about the animal that you want to bring into your home, you will also become aware of the pros and cons of bringing that animal home. This will help you decide if you are really ready for the animal or not and then buy one.

2. Buying from pet stores

Getting rats from a pet store is the equivalent of getting a puppy from a pet store. It is usually not recommended as the rats sold here are usually not bred under the right conditions and can have several issues like tumors or mycoplasma.

There are some pet stores that have strict policies about selling only healthy rats and then there are others that keep the rats in very poor conditions. If a pet store is the only source available to you, then there are some things that you must consider:

- **The living conditions of the rats:** No pet store is interested in housing the animals on a long term basis. Therefore, they seldom invest in large cages with ample space and accessories to keep the rats active. They will use enclosures that are too small and may even have a substrate that is not appropriate. These rats are also never on a good diet. Irrespective of the age and the current physical condition, all the rats are given the same diet. This means that the kittens who need more protein fail to get it and often end up being undersized.

While there are legal requirements with respect to the space available to the animals, most pet stores simply dump several rats in one aquarium. In case of baby rats or kittens, especially, overcrowding is a very common issue.

Domesticated rats are social with human beings. That said, they do need some place to seek refuge and hide from time to time. In pet stores, rats are subject to a lot of disturbance such as people knocking on the glass, children crying or screaming or even just people walking to and fro. Without any space to hide from this commotion, the rats tend to get extremely stressed.

In the younger rats, extreme stress can lead to compromised immunity which means that they are vulnerable to several health issues. These pet stores do not provide any hiding area for the fear of the rats being cooped up there all day. This may lead to loss of customers as they are unable to interact with the rats. However, for the rats, these living conditions can spell disaster with respect to their health.

Investing in these rats means that you could be investing in a rat with multiple health issues as well as possible behavioral troubles as well.

- **Poor breeding:** The objective with breeding in most commercial set ups is to produce as many rats as possible in the shortest span of time. This leaves very little room to think about proper breeding conditions. As a result, rats produced in rodent mills often live in horrendous conditions.

They are kept in crammed housing areas in cages that are similar to the ones used in laboratories. Females are continuously pregnant. This is because they are always housed with males, which makes them capable of becoming pregnant immediately after giving birth to a litter.

As a result, the offspring are usually unhealthy and undersized as the mother's body is unable to provide them with the nutrition that they need.

In these breeding conditions, the kittens are never handled by people. The only time they are handled is when they reach the pet store or in some cases, when they go to their new home. This means that you have a rat who is not used to human touch, increasing the chances of bites because the rat feels threatened when handled.

The mother rats usually die very young as they are not cared for properly. They are never given any stimulation or exercise and are only expected to constantly produce litters. The food given to these rats is sub-standard, especially when you take into consideration the rich nutrition required by a pregnant female.

When you go to a pet store, you must enquire about the source of their rats. Many pet stores will make claims of getting their rats from local breeders. They may also insist that only a few litters are produced each year and that the rats are bred in healthy conditions. This could be true in some cases but not all.

To confirm, you can ask to meet the breeder that they are sourcing the rats from. In the case of genuine pet stores, there should be no hesitation when it comes to introducing you to the breeder. However, those who source their rats from rodent mills will have several excuses not to let you meet the breeder that they work with.

While the poor living conditions and breeding conditions are a concern a bigger concern is the quality of the rats that are produced. With genuine breeders, the healthiest rats are chosen for breeding. They also consider the temperament of the rat before choosing to breed them.

They also take into consideration things like genetic lines that have lived the longest. In rodent mills, the male and the female are just dumped into a cage with no such considerations at all.

There is no thought given to what they may be breeding into the offspring, the health issues in parents or behavioral troubles. In commercial set ups, time is one commodity that is not available. When breeding selectively, breeders will spend a lot of time understanding each genetic line and picking the best from it. With rodent mills, the only consideration is making a profit irrespective of whether the litter develop health issues in the long run.

- **The people that the rats are sold to:** With pet stores, it is impossible to screen and monitor the people whom the rats are sold to. Any reputable breeder will make sure that a thorough housing check and background check is done before the rats are sold to a new home. They will also insist that you return the rats to them in case you are unable to take care of them for some reason.

With reputable breeders, there are usually long waiting lists that may require you to wait for months before you get your rat home. This also gives potential owners enough time to interact with rats and learn all about them. That way, you will know if you are truly prepared for the responsibility.

A good breeder, unlike a pet store, will want to stay in touch with every family that he has sold pets to. He will also insist on information such as the age that the rat lives up to in order to maintain proper records such as the lifespan of each line that is produced.

On the other hand, if you have the money, a pet store will sell a rat to you. They are not interested in staying in touch. They may ask you a few basic questions at best but are not really concerned about where the rats end up.

The better pet stores advocate ideas like buying rats in pairs. However, if you can insist that you have one at home even when you do not, there will not be any check or visit to confirm.

With pet stores, there are no restrictions about when you can breed the animals from the time of purchase. Most people who buy these rats are interested in breeding them and making some profits for themselves. It is great if these rats end up with genuine breeders. However, they often end up with those who are only interested in the commercial aspect of it. The primary reason for this is that anyone who is genuinely interested in breeding rats will not purchase undernourished rats from pet stores as the condition will only become worse with each generation.

If you have the chance to talk to people who rescue animals, you will notice that most rats that come to these shelters are originally from pet stores. Those that are purchased from good breeders seldom have any behavioral or health issues. Even when they do, they are often returned to the breeder instead of ending up in a shelter.

- **Pet stores selling top eared and dumbo rats:** One of the most recent phenomenons in pet stores is selling dumbos and top eared rats as different species. They are the same and go by the scientific name *rattusnorvegicus.* There is a difference in the position of the ears which is the result of mutation due to interbreeding. This also ends up in misinformation such as Dumbos and other fancy rats being incompatible.

  This approach has made people view the Dumbo as some exotic species while it is nothing more than the regular domesticated rat. Pet stores may sell them at much higher costs and even make claims of Dumbos living longer than the other fancy rats.

  Even if a pet store insists that they source from a good breeder, make sure that you double check. Any good breeder is aware of the poor conditions that rats are kept in at pet stores and will seldom sell to a pet store. Just as breeders of top class dogs will not sell to pet stores, neither do breeders who produce healthy fancy rats.

3. Adopting pet rats

The third option available to you if you want to bring home a pet rat is adoption. There are several rats that are abandoned for several reasons from the owners being unable to care for it or sudden behavioral or health issues that they were unable to deal with. However, when adopting rats from shelters, you need to be an experienced rat owner or should be able to get some assistance from someone who knows how to handle rats and deal with them correctly.

There are several shelters that are dedicated exclusively to rodents and small animals. You will be able to find the details of all the shelters in your locality with the rat and mouse clubs in your state. Alternatively, you can even check with shelter that you know of to find rats that need a permanent home.

There are some guidelines with respect to adopting a rat. Here are a few tips that will help beginners or those with prior experience to adopt a rat:

- Spend some time at the shelter learning about the different rats that are available. You should pick one that has the right temperament for your home. That is the priority and next is the health of the rat. If you are able to care for rats that are unwell or have some genetic issues, then may choose one that really needs your help.

- There is an adoption application with most shelters that you will have to fill out. The application will require all your contact details and also some information about your home and lifestyle to check if you are a suitable adopter.

- You can submit these forms online unless there are documents that you have to submit along with the application. In that case you can either drop them off at the shelter or send them by post.

- There is a mandatory interview process for each candidate before the rat is given to you. The objective is to understand the purpose of adoption and also the experience that you have with keeping rats and handling them.

- The rescue shelter will make recommendations based on the interview. They may refuse to let you adopt a certain rat for some valid reasons. For instance, if a rat is not comfortable with children, they may not allow you to adopt it if you have children at home. The idea is to ensure that the rat does not have to go through this process of adoption yet again.

- A fee of up to $10 or £5 is charged for adoption. This is mostly to cover the expenses borne by the shelter towards the rat. However, in some cases, there may be no fee at all or the fee may be higher as per the care given to the rat.

Most shelters insist that you return the rat to the shelter if you are unable to take proper care. Some of them may also conduct house visits after adoption to make sure that the rats are in good condition.

It is best that you pay a visit to the shelter instead of choosing the rats online. This will give you valuable tips about handling the rats and learning to care for them. Most shelters also have open "meet and greet" days that encourage people to adopt rats and give them a permanent home. Signing up for the newsletters of shelters will give you all the information that you need about these special events.

4. Choosing the perfect pet rat

There are some guidelines to choosing the ideal pet rat. This will make sure that you only bring home one that you are able to provide good care to. A healthy rat that is compatible with your household and your lifestyle will also make it more comfortable and pleasurable to have one in your home.

Health and behavior

When you are scouting for rats, here are a few pointers that will give you a few hints about the health and general behavior of the rat:

- The fur should be even and clean. Any matting or bald spots is an indication of poor health.

- The cages should be well maintained. Most of the health issues with rats are the result of improper sanitation.

- The rats should have clear and alert eyes. There should not be any clouding or signs of discharge near the eyes.

- The ears should have clean edges and should not show any signs of deformity.

- There should be no nasal discharge.

- The feet should be free from wounds or abscesses. The padding should be clean and the skin on the padding must be intact.

- Make sure you interact with the rats. When you approach a rat, they may either try to run away or may show some curiosity with sniffs and licks. Choose the latter. If you fall in love with a rat who is evidently shy and scared, you can still being them home if you are willing to be patient and give them time to get used to you.

Male or female?

Like any other species of animals, male and female rats have different temperaments and will be very different as pets. Usually, it is recommended that you bring home a pair of rats. However, if you are willing to spend enough time with your rat, even one is a good idea. The basic idea is to ensure that they have enough socialization as rats rely on good company for good health.

In case you decide to buy more than one rat, then you need to make sure that they are of the same gender or that the females have been spayed and that the males have been neutered. This will prevent chances of unexpected litters. Male and females have some great qualities although they are evidently different from one another.

With males, you will see that they are more laid back. They are great if you are looking for a rat who likes to snuggle and be a lap-rat. Male rats do get territorial. So, it is a good idea to bring one home that is 4 months of age or younger to make the introduction into your home less stressful.

It is common for the males to mark their territory. They do this with small sprays of urine around the cage. Usually, a male rat will be larger in size in comparison to a female.

Female rats on the other hand are extremely energetic and love to play. They will get into your stuff at every opportunity that they get even if the room is fully rat-proofed. This high energy and extreme curiosity about everything around them makes it impossible to get them to cuddle. However, once every while, you may be able to get one of them to calm down for a few seconds for a quick snuggle.

Unlike males, females are more accepting of new females in their cage. They do not leave scent marks in the cage. However, they may dribble from time to time. Females are smaller and as they age, they tend to calm down and become great lap rats.

No matter what the gender of the rat is, you can be assured of a great time with your pet. They are extremely loving and will reciprocate perfectly to a little bit of love and care.

All you need to do is learn to handle them well and give them some of your time.

Chapter 3: Preparing for a Pet Rat

Once you know where you want to buy your pet rat from, you need to make sure that your home is a suitable environment to bring the rat into. You need to make ample preparations before you actually bring the rat home. If you are scrambling for supplies and to find a decent housing area for the rat after he is in your home, then it increases the stress of getting acquainted with a new environment for your pet.

1. Pet Rat housing

When it comes to housing, there are several options that are available. In this section we will discuss the pros and cons of each type of housing that is popularly chosen for pet rats.

No matter what you choose, here are a few things that you need to keep in mind with respect to the housing area of the rat:

- There should be ample space for all the rats that are housed in the cage.

- The cage should be safe for the rat. This means that the locks should be sturdy and should prevent any chances of escapes.

- Always buy the largest cage that you can afford.

- Cleanliness is of utmost importance to rats. So you need to have good bedding material and a litter box to keep the cage clean.

While we will be discussing all the possible housing options for rats, note that storage bins, habitrails and aquariums should never be chosen as permanent housing areas for rats. They can be uncomfortable for the rat after some time for several reasons that we will discuss in the following section.

What are the different housing options?

The most popular housing options for rats include:

- **Cages:** You can get a range of different designs, sizes and costs with wired cages. They are available in pet stores as well as online. Usually, most rat owners prefer the wired cages. You can choose one with bar spacing as per the size of the rat and the age of the rat. Typically, it is possible to use a ferret cage for larger female rats and the males. In the case of the younger rats, you will need spacing that will keep them from escaping or getting stuck between the bars.

There are several advantages to choosing wired cages for rats. One of the most important things is that it is well ventilated. There is no risk of ammonia fumes with these cages. They also provide ample space for ramps, to create different levels and to hang toys and accessories to keep the rat stimulated. In addition to that, it is also easier to interact with rats through these cages.

There are some disadvantages to wired cages as well. Most of the food and the litter tends to fall on the floor with this type of housing. They may also cause foot injuries and conditions like bumblefoot. You can either place needlepoint mesh, linoleum or cloth on the floor of the cage to prevent this issue.

When choosing a wired cage, make sure that you opt for powder coated ones. They are also easier to clean and do not cause zinc poisoning in rats as opposed to the galvanized steel wire cages.

- **Aquariums:** You can find several sizes and heights with aquariums. If you plan to use an aquarium, make sure that it has a cover to avoid any chances of escapes. You will require special water bottles that can hang down from the sides of the aquarium. While an aquarium is never a good choice for permanent housing, you need to make sure that you get one that is at least 40-60 gallons in length if you want to house a pair of rats.

There are several owners who prefer to use an aquarium because it is much easier to clean. The bedding, food and the litter stays in the housing area and does not fall on the ground. For those who have multiple rats, a cage will require more space. Aquariums also keep drafts away.

But there are more cons than pros with respect to an aquarium. They do not provide ample space for the rats. They can cause overheating in the rats. They lead to condensation and also breakage issues. One of the biggest hazards with aquariums is accumulation of ammonia fumes. Glass is also more prone to breaking which makes it an unsafe enclosure for your pet rat.

- **Combo cages:** The other option is to use a wired cage that fits on top of an aquarium to make a combo cage. These cages are not easily available in pet stores and you will have to look online. The advantage with these cages is that they provide ample ventilation and height to the rats. When you are breeding rats, these cages are valuable as they provide a basement area that is free from drafts and noise. It also gives the mother rat some space to rest for a while and get some much needed solitude.

- **Homemade cabinets:** These cages are also called grotto cages and make a great choice for housing rats. You will need some raw material and some tools to customize the housing area for your rats.

  The best thing about this type of housing is that you can keep the area much tidier in comparison to a cage. You can create as many levels as you like and also make ample space to keep the environment of the rat stimulating.

  The downside to using a cabinet cage is that it is too heavy. It makes it harder to take this type of housing outdoors for periodic cleaning and full sterilization incase there are signs of parasites or illnesses.

  One option is to add wheels to the cabinet to make it easier to move around. You need to make sure that the wood is protected. If not, urine can be soaked up into the wood making it very unpleasant for the rats to live in these housing areas. In addition to that, these housing areas are also prone to weather related damage. Do not forget about the sharp teeth of your rats that will help them chew right through the cage and make a run for it.

- **Bin housing:** You can use modified bins such as large sterilized bins as housing areas for your rats. This is one of the most popular choices among breeders. You can find several tips to modify these bins on the Internet.

  The advantages to using bins is that they are easy to clean. You can also reduce the space used by stacking the bins up. They are easier to store when they are not in use. Most importantly, they keep the bedding material and the litter from falling on the floor around the enclosure.

The disadvantages include minimized interactions with the owners. These storage bins also make it hard for the rat to climb and stay active. You do not have enough space to include toys or wheels for your rat. The floor space is also much lesser with these storage bins. Unless you can cut out air holes or pockets in the storage bin it restricts ventilation making the housing area unsafe for the rats.

No matter which of the housing areas you choose from the ones mentioned above, make sure that you keep the environment stimulating. You should also choose a housing area that keeps the rats healthier for longer.

Accessorizing the cage
Once the cage has been set up, you need to make it comfortable for the rat to live in. He will be spending most of his time in the cage and, hence, requires an environment that is stimulating as well.

You can outfit the cage of your rat in many ways to make it more interesting. There are store bought items as well as homemade accessories that you can use for the cage. You can also look for accessories that are commonly used in cases of birds, ferrets and other smaller animals in local pet stores.

Here are some accessories that you must include in the rat cage:

Bedding and nesting
A large part of the rat's day includes lounging around and sleeping. So, they need a warm bed and some elevated lounging spots. They need a nesting box that will let him hide and sleep. There are several things that you can find that will make for a cozy hiding space such as roll-a-nest beds, igloos, log cabin homes, chinchilla bath houses and more.

If you want to craft something at home, you can also use an inverted bowl with a hole drilled in it, PVC pipes, large sturdy cardboard boxes or even plastic boxes that are used for storage. All you have to do is drill some holes in them and they are good to go.

Once you have figured out the hiding spots, they will also need good bedding. Rats usually make a nest of their own with the material available. They enjoy setting up beds on their own. The best material that you can use include CareFresh bedding, paper towels, fabrics without strings or frayed edges and shredded paper.

This bedding material should be changed regularly, preferably every morning. If the urine is soaked into the bedding material and allowed to stay for a long time, it can be harmful to the rat. The urine releases ammonia fumes that cause several health issues.

You will also have to provide some elevated escape areas for the rats as they love to stay high off the floor. There are several pet supply brands that make sleeping tubes, hammocks and hanging hideaways.

A hammock is a must have for your rat cage. You can find one in any size. If you have a wired cage, the advantage is that you have plenty of space to hang these beds in.

You can even make soft tubes and hammocks at home. You can sew one in any fancy design that you like. If sewing is not something that you are interested in, then you can even use cloth place mats, scrap fabric, cloth diapers and towels to fashion the hammock with. A soft tube can be made with the legs of your pants cut out and hung in the cage.

You can hang these hammocks with hooks or chains or just about anything that keeps them secure. You must also line the soft tube or a towel to make it easier for you to clean them out from time to time.

Pet stores will also be able to provide you with hard tubes that are actually meant for ferrets. These long tubes are hung with hooks and chains. They are transparent and come in several colors. You can make a hard tube at home with PVC pipes that you can drill a hole in and hang in the cage.

Flooring of the cage
If you have a wired cage, especially, getting the right flooring material is very important. You will have to cover the whole floor with some material that can protect the feet of your rats. Very often, rats can sprain their legs or even break them if the foot gets caught in the cage floor.

If the wire spacing on the floor is about ½ an inch, these injuries can be reduced. Wired floors can also increase the chances of bumblefoot and can aggravate the condition if it already exists.

You have several options to make the floor of the cage safe. One of the best options is linoleum. Choose the non-glued type to make cleaning easier. This flooring material also looks very clean and attractive. You have several other options like shelf liners, non-stick rubber, needlepoint canvas or cloth.

It is best to avoid flooring material like carpet, plywood and cardboard. They are very hard to clean and it is impossible to just wipe them down on a daily basis to keep them well maintained.

Feeding and watering bowls
Rats need constant food supply as they are free feeders. The food dishes that you use should be low and heavy to prevent food from being spilled on the floor. You have two options with the food dish. You can get one that you mount on the side of the wall or use a food hopper that will dispense food regularly.

Any wet or perishable food that you give the rat should be placed in a separate bowl. Sometimes, rats tend to stash their food. If you have such a rat at home, make sure you remove the perishable food before it decomposes.

Rats require a lot of water. So it is important to have clean drinking water in the cage at all times. Never put the water in a bowl that is open. Rats tend to fill them with bedding or may just tip them over.

You have the option of using water bottles in the cage. They can be mounted on the cage on the outside and have a sipper tube that passes through the mesh. In case of open cages, the top of these bottles should be protected using an empty can or bowl to keep the rats from chewing them.

Having multiple sources of water is recommended. That way, if there is a leak in one bottle or the bottle is not refilled, they will still have ample water to drink. If you are using an aquarium, make sure that you get a bottle holder that you can hang from the side of the cage. This will keep the bottle protected from chewing. The seal of the bottle should be in place at all times to prevent dripping. This bottle should be fully sanitized each week.

Ledges and shelves
Having multiple levels in the cage keeps the rats entertained. You can use several things from baskets, ferret hammocks to bird platforms to make these levels in the cage. You can even connect ferret tubes and attach them on the top of the cage or on the side. These tubes act as ramps for the rats to get from one level to the other. Coated wire shelving can also be used by cutting it to fit into the cage.

Wire baskets also make great shelves. You can suspend these baskets in the center of the cage. If the cage is small, you can also use cable ties to attach the basket to the side of the cage.

Toys for rats
Rats are extremely intelligent creatures and will require a lot of mental stimulation in order to be healthy. This can be done with the help of several toys that can either be bought or made at home.

Some of the most important types of toys are:

- Wheels: Having an exercise wheel in the cage will keep your rat engaged when you are unable to spend enough time with him. It is believed that female rats are more inclined towards running. This is not always true, though. Sometimes, even the makes use them. Make sure that the rat wheel that you use is not the wired type. Using a plastic wheel or a metal wheel will prevent any injuries to the legs or the feet as they do not get caught while the rat is running.

- Treat toys: These toys are easily the most favored types of toys. You can find several options in pet stores including hanging treat balls, Pick-a-Peanut, Bounce Back Rat Toy and more. You can also make a treat toy at home by placing some treats inside a cardboard box. Your rat will have a blast demolishing these boxes in the quest for the treats. Hard treats or fruits can also be suspended in the cage with the help of binder rings. The rat will love to nibble at these hard treats from time to time and will keep himself engaged.

- Climbing toys: Climbing is a great form of exercise for your rat. There are several options like climbing tubes, ladders, ropes and bird branches that you can use. There are several climbing toys available in the bird and ferret department at pet stores. If you have rats that are elderly or unwell, climbing toys should not be used as it can cause a lot of stress to them.

- Digging boxes: It is instinctive for rats to dig and forage. You can give them a digging box to keep this natural behavior alive. To make a digging box all you will need is a plastic box or a litter box. You can even use a small plastic storage box. Pour in some sterile potting soil into the box. Make sure that the soil is free from any pesticides or chemicals. Then, you can grow wheat grass, rye or oat grass in this soil. Make sure you provide enough moisture for these plants to grow but not so much that there is growth of mold and fungus. You can create a more natural ambience by placing buried PVC tunnels and assorted rocks. Hide some treats in the digging box to make it even more fun. You can keep this digging box inside or outside the cage. If it is kept inside the cage, you need to clean the soil on a regular basis.

Where to place the cage
The placement of the cage is crucial. The better care you taking in choosing the area you will house the rat in, the easier it will be for him to get used to his new home.

The cage should be free from any heavy draft and direct sunlight. While air movement is good for rats, too much draft from a window, air conditioning or a table fan can affect the body temperature of the rats adversely.

The room that you place the cage in should be fully dark at night. Rats require some amount of complete darkness without which their health, particularly reproductive health, is adversely affected.

The temperature of the room plays a very important role in the well-being of the rat. The temperature of the room should be between 72-80 degrees Fahrenheit. This will keep the rat comfortable. If the temperature is too high or too low, rats tend to get very stressed. This will lead to several health issues. During the breeding season, it is advised to keep the temperature between 75 and 78 degree Fahrenheit.

It is a good idea to place the cage on a table or a stand instead of placing it on the floor directly. Also remember that an area that allows maximum interactions with you will keep your rat very happy. Once the spot is chosen, you have to make sure that the housing fits into it properly. For those who live in an apartment, it is also necessary to be able to fit the cage into the shower area. This is because you will most probably not have access to any area where you can use a hose to clean the cage thoroughly.

The housing area that you choose for the rat should be comfortable for you and the rat. You should be able to access the cage easily to take the feeding and watering bowls out every day to clean and refill them. You should also be able to get the bedding and other dirt out of the cage conveniently. But most importantly, you should be able to interact with the rats easily and even be able to keep an eye on them at all times of the day.

2. Rat proofing your home
Once your rat has been trained, you may want to leave him out of the cage from time to time. Then again, there may be some instances when he escapes from the cage and gets into your stuff. Rat proofing your house and the room that you will keep the cage in is necessary to make sure that

your rat is safe. It will also keep the rat from destroying your things. Everyone knows how notorious rats are for chewing up stuff.

Top five hazards for rats
There are several things in the house that can hurt the rat. But, of all these things there are five top hazards that you need to protect your pet from:

1. Electrical cords

Whether they are plugged in or not, any cord that is attached to a stereo, TV, computer, lamps and other equipment is a serious hazard. If the cord is plugged in and your rat chews on it, chances are that he will get electrocuted. Even when the cord is unplugged, chewing on it will leave it damaged and frayed. Then, the cord becomes dangerous to use. You need to replace any cord that has been exposed by chewing.

There are two simple solutions to this hazard:

• Make sure that every cord is unplugged. If this is the solution you choose, you will have to follow through every time and ensure that every single cord has been unplugged each time you leave the house.

• Keep the cords covered. There are metal and plastic tubes that can be purchased in hardware stores. Even when the cords have been covered fully, you need to keep an eye out every time the rat is out to make sure that they do not chew right through the cover that you have used. That is why metal covers are the best options for rat proofing.

2. Crack and crevices
Any crack or gap under the door or under cabinets, heater vents and screens in the windows are hazardous. There may be multiple nooks in the furniture which can not only hurt the rat but may also cause damage to the furniture. There are different things that you can do depending on where the cracks are present to get rid of potential hoarding spots and hideouts.

Furniture:
Any opening underneath the sofa gives the rat ample space to crawl in and hide in the tight space. It is very hard to get them out of these spaces. Another hazard is if the rat hides in the cushion and someone sits on it, crushing him or severely injuring him.

A mattress box spring can make a great nest building area as the rat can chew into it easily. It is almost impossible to get the rat out of this spot.

If a rat gets under a rocker or lounge chair, they can be crushed to death when you move it while they are underneath.

In addition to this, the inside of furniture contains several tacks, sharp ends and other material that can lead to puncture wounds. The solution to these issues are:

- Any dangerous furniture should be removed or covered with a bedspread or old sheet.

- Any entrance under the furniture should be blocked. You can use corrugated cardboard to wrap these openings as they are harder to chew through.

Doors and windows
Any crack under the door or window is dangerous, especially if it opens into the outdoors or into a garage. Even the smallest crevice is enough for the rat to crawl through. They are very skilled at squeezing through small cracks and crevices to get out. The solutions to these cracks and crevices are:
- All cracks that are more than ¼ inches in width should be blocked. This can be done by just wedging cardboard into the space.

- For the space underneath the door, install a door sweep to close the gap that the rat can escape through.

- If you have any sliding door or window, it can make a great getaway even if it is slightly open. Make sure that every window and sliding door is closed when the rat is out of the cage.

Cabinets and drawers
There are several gaps at the bottom of cabinets where the base of the cabinet meets the floor. These gaps lead to the inside of the wall where the rats can chew the wiring of your house or even get lost. This can be prevented by:
- Checking for any openings under the cabinets with your fingers and then covering them with cardboard or any material that can keep the rats out.

Heater vents
These vents also lead to the inside of the wall and can be very dangerous when they are on. You need to block these vents completely to prevent your rat from getting in and hurting himself.

3. Dangling blinds cords, curtain, blanket and bedspread fringes

Anything that is dangling or loose is a toy for your rat. Just like cats, rats find them extremely amusing. However, when they are left unsupervised, they can get tangled and may lose circulation to the area that is tangled. Usually the limbs get caught, leading to a loss of the limb.

The best way to prevent these accidents is to make sure that you remove anything with fringes from the room. Any cords that are dangling can be folded and put out of the rat's reach.

4. Toilets

Rats can jump onto a toilet seat and fall into the bowl. They cannot swim and will drown if not taken out on time. If your rat has easy access to the bathroom, the lid of the toilet must remain closed at all times.

5. Garbage cans

Rats and garbage are two peas in a pod! Rats love to explore what is inside the garbage can. This means that they can end up eating something that is dangerous for them. They can also get stuck in the garbage can if it has a lid. The only solution to this is to keep the garbage can out of the rat's way. You can alternatively place something heavy on the lid so that the rat is unable to open it and get in.

Preparing the room as per the rat's personality

The damage caused to your room depends entirely on the personality of the rat. This also determines what the rat will find most attractive and what he will try to get into first. For instance, some rats are chewers while others are climbers. The priority of rat proofing will change as per the personality of the animal.

If the rat is a chewer

The risk of injuries is very high if your rat likes to chew stuff. They can get electrocuted or may be poisoned. In addition to that, a lot of damage can be caused to your stuff. They will gnaw on the plaster on the wall, paint, wooden material, papers, books, bedspreads, electrical cords and just about anything that catches their eye.

There are some solutions that you can apply if you have a chewer on your hands:

- Keep all the cords and furniture protected as discussed above.

- Give the rat a lot of chew toys. There are ones that are made especially for small animals and can be placed in different areas of the room.

- Behavior modification exercises are needed. You can designate a certain sound or cue to tell the rat that you do not approve of some behavior. A sharp no or a clicking sound works really well. Just when they begin to chew on something make the sound. You need to redirect the rat immediately for him to understand what is out of limits.

- Keep the plants in your house out of the rats reach. There several plants that can be toxic to the rat when chewed upon.

- If there are any bits of food on the floor, they need to be cleaned out immediately. You must also get rid of paper, bugs and other things that can end up on the floor or in the carpet.

- Your beds and furniture should be covered with a blanket or sheet. This will prevent chewing and any possible stains that are left due to the marking behavior of the rat.

- If your rat is attracted to one particular spot in the house that he chews on, you can even place a bitter apple or something that is unpleasant in taste or smell but safe for the rat. You can find these products in pet stores and online as well. They can be placed on wooden objects and also on the walls. When your rat approaches these areas to chew on them, the bitter apple or any other product that you have used will keep them away.

If the rat is a climber
In general rats are great climbers. Some are more inclined to climbing than others. They will get on top of bookshelves, curtains, towel racks, shower doors, cabinets or any space that allows them to find a good hold and climb. Once they are up, they will try to get as high as they can. Sadly, they do not know how to get back to the ground safely and may end up falling and injuring themselves in most cases.

Here are some solutions that you can apply if your rat is a climber:
- Keep an eye on the rat when he is out of the cage. If he gets to any space that is at a height, make sure you are close to them to catch them if they start to fall.

- Limit access to areas that the rat can climb onto. Observe the behavior of your rat to see what areas need to be off limits.

- Safe climbing areas can be created using fabric to cover a wall, ladder toys or even anything that slopes and ends in a safe ramp. This will create an indoor playground of sorts for your rat. It is very stimulating and also makes sure that the rat can engage his climbing skills and also climb down to safety when he is not under the supervision of his owner.

If the rat is a jumper

Jumping is yet another common behavior associated with rats. They will try to jump from the bookshelf on to the table or even jump from one shelf to the next one that is higher up. In the process, they can fall from a great height and have serious injuries. There are chances of broken bones, bruising of the internal organs and, in worst cases, death.

The only solution with jumpers is to keep an eye on them when they are out of the cage. They should be watched closely whenever they start to explore a new room. You can even move the furniture around to make sure that they do not jump off or are safe even if they decide to do so. The most effective way, however, is to make sure that you are always there to catch the rat if you feel like he is losing his grip and is about to fall.

If the rat is a urine marker

This is a very common problem that you will face with male rats. They will dribble urine in different parts of the house to mark their territory. This can leave undesirable stains and also a stench around the house.

Some solutions that may work with urine markers are:
- Behavior modification techniques can be used to divert this behavior. You can do this by arranging litter boxes outside your cage. When you see the rat marking, catch him and put him into the litter box. You can also take him first to the litter box before allowing him to explore a room or play there. This will reinforce the fact that you want him to urinate in that area.

- Neutering the male rat is an effective way to keep this territorial behavior at bay and prevent marking altogether.

Overall rat safety

No matter what the personality of your rat is, you can take a few simple steps that will make it safe for him to be outside the cage. To begin with, place the cage of the rat in the room that you allocate for his play. Whenever you let the rat out, make sure that the door of the cage is open so that he can come back when he wants.

Rats generally go back to the cage to urinate and defecate. However, in the initial period, it will help to place litter boxes around the room that they are going to be playing in. Once they get used to the designated area in the cage to relieve themselves, you can reduce the number of boxes that you place around the room.

If you do notice that the rat continues to urinate or defecate outside the cage, you will also notice that they choose only some spots, mostly the corners. You can simply place a litter box in these areas or even in areas that you want them to use. If they do have accidents outside the litter box and you catch them in time, take them to the litter box to help them understand what you expect from them.

Before you let the rat out in the room freely, it is a good idea to clean and vacuum the space. Rats are known for eating just about anything. This can sometimes also include old and spoiled pieces of food, bugs or paper that can make the rat sick or even cause injuries.

In general, whenever the rat is allowed to explore a room, you need to keep a close eye on them. You need to observe every move of the rat to make sure that they do not get into anything that is dangerous. In some cases you may not even expect some area to be harmful and the rat may injure himself in the process of exploring it.

There may be some areas in your house that you find really hard to close off and prevent the rat from entering them. In that case, you can simply place some plastic bags around the area. When the rat moves on the bag, you will hear the sound and will be able to monitor them closely or just take them out of the area right away to prevent injuries.

While there are many things you can do to rat proof the house, you can never make it 100% safe for the animal. Rats are small and delicate. This makes them prone to many accidents. So, never let the rat out of the cage if you do not have someone to supervise the rat. This is especially true when you have other pets at home or if there are children at home. Keeping an eye on them at all times is the only way to keep them perfectly safe. You may also not want to let the rat out till you have learnt to handle them well. This can make it hard to get them out of danger in time. If the rat does get away by mistake, you can use treats to lure him back into the cage if you are unsure about picking them up.

After you are finished with the play session, set the rat back in the cage and then make sure that the door is fully secure. Rats have a way of getting into trouble because of their innate curious nature.

It is up to you to think ahead and keep them safe.

Chapter 4: After the Rat is Home

Once your pet rat is home, you need to make sure that you give him the right ambience at least for the initial days to keep him comfortable. That way, he will not feel any additional stress while making the transition.

Once the rat is home, you need to take complete responsibility of his care which means that the rat needs to be fed, groomed and also given a lot of mental and physical stimulation to maintain his health.

If you already have a mischief of rats in your house who are established, making introductions is the key to keeping your rats comfortable. When it comes to your other pets such as cats and dogs, you have to be very cautious to prevent any chances of mishaps.

1. The rat's first day at home

A new rat is a new member in your family. Even if it is as affordable and non-demanding as the rat, you have to make sure that you make them feel as comfortable as possible in their new home. The first day is important right from the time you drive from the shelter or the breeder's to your home.

Travelling with your rat

A carrier should be prepared when you go to pick your rat up, no matter how long or short the drive is. Many pet stores will just put the rat in a box and hand them to you. This is not a safe option. You can get a cat carrier that is good enough or you may use a wired cage. Do not take an aquarium along as it may shatter if there is any slip or fall. The best option is a plastic carrier. You can get a small one as the larger one is expensive. You can even make a wooden travel cage if you have the necessary skills for it.

The easiest thing to do for a homemade travel cage is to get a plastic storage box and drill a couple of holes in the lid and the sides.

The substrate that you put in this travel box should be safe and light. The best option is to use plain paper towels. In case the trip is long, you can use pelleted paper litter for more absorption. Make sure you carry some treats along to help the rat stay relaxed. Do not place the water bottle inside the cage. This may lead to spills when the vehicles moves. You can give the rat some water to drink whenever you stop the car. Fresh vegetables make great treats for rats when travelling.

When you take your rat from the breeders, ask for some litter or bedding material from the cage that he was in. This will make the rat more comfortable because he has some familiar scents around him. If you are

46

picking up a pair of rats, then they are a lot more comfortable as they have a familiar cage mate with them.

Never let the rat out of the cage till you are home. The rat may get spooked or may try to escape into corners inside the vehicle or make his way out of the window. The door of the carrier should be shut tight throughout the trip.

It is possible that the rat gets a little nervous or excited as the vehicle begins to move. However, this dies out in about half an hour and the rat will fall asleep. Rats can stay for as long as 8 hours in a car provided that they are given enough food and water.

The first night at home
Even if you bring home a rat that is used to being handled by people from the time he is born, a new environment will take some time for him to gain the trust of people. Usually, rats that have been brought home from a pet store will have more trouble getting used to a new environment as they are not used to being handled correctly.

You can, however, make this transition a lot easier for your new pet. The cage should be placed in a room that is quiet and free from too many bright lights. The other pets in your home including cats, dogs or ferrets should not be let into this room. These animals are predators and will make the rat very nervous and uncomfortable. Even a rat who is seemingly calm will become nervous and extremely stressed. Having a toy or some bedding material from the pet store or from the breeder's will help make the rat more comfortable.

Allow the rat to take his time to become comfortable in your home. Do not rush the interaction. You can just spend some time near the cage or just keep the door open and wait for the rat to approach you. Rats tend to get attached to their cages and will try to scurry back every time you take them out, especially in the initial days.

You can encourage the rat to come to you using a few treats. Try to pet him while he is still in the cage. If he resists, let it go and try again when he is calmer. There are several treats like frozen vegetables, cereal or yoghurt based treats that the rat will be drawn to immediately. If they come to you at the sight of the treat, just set it down and get your hand out of the way. When you build enough trust and the rat is assured that you mean no harm, he will be willing to take the treat from your hand.

When the rat becomes comfortable outside the cage, you can introduce him to other play areas. Keep these areas restricted. You can choose the couch or the bed, keeping them covered fully to avoid any burrowing or staining from urination. A smaller room is ideal for play with the new rat. Rats are most comfortable in an area that is dim and lowly lit. So, keeping the room dark or throwing some cover over you and the rat will help. This will keep him at ease.

As the rat gets more comfortable, his play will also get more energetic and will usually include some amount of bouncing and jumping. They also nip when they jump, just like cats. This is gentle and will not hurt you. Do not punish your rat for displaying this behavior.

This is a sign that your rat is getting more comfortable with you and views you as a playmate. They will also lick at times. This grooming behavior shows that he is comfortable with you and is accepting of you. They will also chatter and grind their teeth to show comfort. They display this behavior when they are happy.

Quarantining the rat
Quarantining your new rat is very important. Unlike other pets such as cats and dogs, there are no vaccinations available for rats. This means that any contagious disease can spread in an instant. So, keeping a sick rat away from healthy ones is a must.

Your new rat can put the health of your gerbil, hamster, mice or any other rodent at risk. Pets like cats and dogs do not contract diseases from rats usually. There are two primary viruses that your rat may carry. They are the Sendai and the SDA virus. These viruses cause respiratory infections.

A rat can simply be a carrier of these viruses without any symptoms of the associated disease. So, a rat that looks healthy is not a rat that does not put the health of your other rodents at risk. However, they will die when they run the course and do not have any new host to infect. A rat that has had any disease caused by these viruses will be immune. This is why you need to quarantine the rat correctly.

These viruses are airborne, so your new rat and other rodents should not share the air supply. This is possible when you keep them in a different building altogether. If that is not possible, make sure that you separate them as much as you can. Keep them in separate rooms that are at a good distance from one another.

You will need to wash your hands every time you handle the new rat. Your hands must be cleaned with a strong disinfectant before you handle the other rodents in your home, the accessories in their cage or their toys. These viruses can also remain potent in your nasal passage for a few hours. So wait for a couple of hours between interactions with your new rat and current rodent pets. It is even better if you can have a friend or relative take care of the new rat for a few days.

The minimum quarantining period is three weeks. If the rat is brought home from a pet store, you can quarantine them for longer, possibly an entire month. During this time, if there are any symptoms of possible diseases, have the rat treated. Then, quarantine the rat for three weeks more after he has recovered fully. The higher the number of new rats, the longer the quarantine period should be. This is because the virus will have multiple hosts that can be infected.

Some symptoms of a new rat
A new rat can have some symptoms that will seem like some health issue or illness. They may sneeze continuously, for instance.

However, in most cases, the rat is not really sick. These symptoms are purely the result of stress. The rat may also be very excited. Since he is getting used to new smells, temperatures, humidity, litter etc, they will show these common symptoms that seem like signs of illnesses.

They will commonly sneeze or may have a red discharge from the nose and the eyes called poryphin. These symptoms are not really something that you need to be too concerned about. Most rats will show these symptoms when they are too excited. The symptoms will diminish as the rat begins to settle in your home

That said, you must make sure that you have the rat thoroughly checked by a vet when he displays any of these symptoms just to be sure that it is nothing serious. Even if it is a health issue, the rat will be in quarantine in this period and is not a threat to your other pets. If the rat has any health issue, make sure that you have it fully treated and then continue the quarantine as mentioned above. That way, all your pets will be completely safe.

There are some symptoms, however, that can be considered a warning sign of potentially serious conditions. These symptoms include lowered body temperature, ruffled fur, loss of appetite, listlessness, labored breathing and paleness. If your rat shows any of these symptoms, he needs to be checked by a vet immediately. You will have to keep in a place that is warm and comfortable. Giving him lots of fluids will also help reduce these symptoms. Then, you need to make sure that he is taken to a vet as soon as possible.

With these simple steps, you can create a positive and comfortable environment for your new furry buddy.

2. Planning introductions

After your new rat has been quarantined fully, you can begin to introduce him to the other rats and rodents. You can follow a few simple steps that will make it easy for them to know each other and get used to one another.

Keep their cages next to each other

Once the quarantine period is complete, you can place the cage of the rats next to one another. The cage should be at enough distance to make sure that they are not able to touch each other. Be very careful about the tail as most people neglect the length added to the body of the rat by the tail.

The rats should be able to see each other and smell each other. This will help them get used to one another. Rats rely largely on their sense of smell. Every rat has a unique smell that lets the other know that they are around. This is one of the reasons why females scent mark the cage when they are placed together with one male in the cage. You will see them scent marking in areas that the other rat may have urinated in. Rats can even mark people because they may smell like another rat to them.

You can keep the cages next to one another for an hour each day for about a week. This will make them more familiar with each other. Rats will be curious about the new member and will continue to look at each other and sniff around. They will show a lot of excitement at times. However, if you notice any hissing or aggressive behavior from either of the rats, you should remember that they are not ready to be in the same cage. In some cases, a certain rat may inherently be unfriendly towards other rats and may not accept a cage mate. That is when you should not force them to be friends as it puts the rats at risk.

Only let them out in a neutral territory

When you see that the rats are comfortable in each other's presence after keeping the cages next to each other, you can proceed to the next step. This is when you start small play dates for your resident rat and the new rat. To make sure that you are able to control any territorial behavior, keep the introduction area neutral. This means that the area should not be used by the resident rats for play.

Some recommended areas to make these introductions are the bathtub or even a couch that the other rats are not allowed on. The bathtub offers and ideal introduction space as it does not have any nooks and crannies and is relatively harder for the rats to climb out of.

You can place them both on a towel with a few treats scattered around. Sharing treats is a great way to make your rats bond with one another.

If the rats are either nervous or jumpy, you can wear a glove and follow the rats around as they play with one another. If they become aggressive, you can separate them quite easily without getting hurt yourself. The glove hand also acts as a great deviation to prevent any unpleasant interactions between your rats. When you see that one rat may become aggressive, just place your hand in between to divert their attention. Since you have the glove to protect you, you will also feel more confident in handling the rats. Any negative confrontation in the initial period makes it harder for the rats to build a good relationship with one another.

Dominance over one another is a very common behavior among rats when they are at play. They will pin each other down, groom each other forcefully or may just push or chase each other. The rat that is submissive will make sharp "eep" sounds that almost sound like he is whispering. This shows that the rat is just giving up or submitting.

While this is normal, being dominant has a lot of significance in the colonies of rats. They may also show dominant behavior when they are sharing a cage. You must intervene if one of the rats squeaks loudly or seems like he is in pain. This means that one of the rats is actually being aggressive. The common signs of aggression are:

- Biting and drawing blood
- Pulling hair out
- Swinging the tail of the other rat around
- Hissing

Make sure you watch your rats at play closely. If you feel like the dominant behavior is going too far, then you should separate them. During the initial introduction, keep these play dates short and not more than 15 minutes long. As the rats get familiar with one another, you will have to intervene less. That is when the time can be increased. If one of the rats is being aggressive repeatedly, you may want to give him some space before you try again.

Putting them together in a familiar territory
When you see that your rats are making progress, you can try to put them together in a familiar territory such as an area of the house that is used by the resident rat to play. This can be the sofa, bed or just about any space that your resident rat is used to.

You will see that the tension between the rats is greater than when they were in a together in a neutral territory. This is when the glove will be very useful. The resident rat will feel the need to protect his territory. As a result, fights to assert dominance will increase quite a bit. Make sure that the rats do not show any violent behavior or aggression. If this behavior escalates, the interaction should be put to an end immediately. You can try again after a few days or even a few hours depending upon the intensity of the bad behavior.

Putting them in the same cage

Once the new rat and the resident rat have formed some sort of bond with one another, they can be made to share the same cage. It is recommended that the rats are put in a new cage altogether. You can also use one of the cages that were used for the initial interactions.

It is definitely less expensive to use a cage that you already have. You will have to make sure that this cage is cleaned thoroughly. You will also have to rearrange the accessories inside the cage. It is a good idea to reserve an entire day to do this. So plan this session when you have the whole day off.

Any old bedding or food should be removed from the cage. You can also use a pet cleaner that will remove any odor from the cage. The cleaning process has to be very thorough. After you have wiped everything down, rearrange the cage fully. For instance, if the cage has multiple levels, the shelves should be moved around. The feeding area and the placement of the water bowls should be changed. If you have hammocks and other detachable items, wash them fully and then place them in a new position.

The idea is to make the cage appear like an entirely new one to both the rats. If the scent of the resident rat persists in the cage, he will try to protect his territory. Cleaning the cage fully will also disorient the rats and avert any aggressive, territorial behavior. This will make both of them engaged in exploring the cage, taking the attention off one another.

Just like the play dates, dominant behavior will be seen when they are placed in the same cage they will take time to settle in and will learn to behave around one another eventually. Boxing and wrestling are part of rat behavior and is no cause for concern. Only when one of the rat vocalizes the pain should you become alert. If you feel like the rats are not getting along, then you can choose to separate them. In most cases, rats love the company of their cage mates and will be cordial and friendly towards one another.

The introduction has a lasting impression on the mind of the rat and will play a big role in the relationship that they build. Making it comfortable and positive will make it easier to get them to like each other.

3. What to feed your rat

Rats are omnivores, which means that a healthy diet consists of both meat and plant based foods. Many people try to feed their rats only vegetarian meals, which does not fulfill their nutritional requirements. Rats need animal protein to live a healthy life.

Feeding rats is relatively easy as they do not fuss over food and will eat just about anything that you give them. Sometimes rats will also eat food just to get over boredom or to feel better when they are unwell.

It is necessary to avoid any sugar when you are feeding your rats. Look for treats that are healthy and nutritionally beneficial to your rats. There are several things that you can include in your rat's diet to add more variety and also keep them healthy.

Commercial food

Commercial foods are generally considered unhealthy and should be given in small portions to your rat. They may contain additives that are very unhealthy for your rat. Some of them also pack in waste foods and chemical food preservatives. If the commercial food contains any traces of corn, there are chances that they develop mold or have fungus in them. Alfalfa pellets that are commonly found in commercial foods are very hard for the rat to digest and may develop health issues.

If you want to include any commercially bought food in your rat's diet, it is a good idea to choose lab blocks. Never give your rat any dog food or cat food. Lab blocks provide the rat with several nutrients that complete his nutritional requirements. Lab blocks are made especially for rats and are easy to find in any pet store or feed stores. There are several brands such as Hagen Nurtiblocks, Mazuri, Oxbow and more that can be included in your rat's diet as a staple food. Another advantage to this is that the teeth do not become overgrown.

Protein intake in rats

Protein is one of the most important nutrients for rats. However, it should be kept within the recommended limit. The diet of your rat should contain up to 18% of proteins. If the rat is pregnant or is nursing, then the content can increase. When rats are given too much protein, they develop protein scabs and also begin to secrete an orange colored grease through the skin. This grease is mostly seen in the male rats.

When you see this grease in the male, they will begin to look unkempt. That is when you need to reduce the protein content in their diet. Instead, you can include more pasta or grains. Bathing them with recommended soaps can also reduce this grease secretion in rats.

There are several sources of proteins such as chicken, turkey, ham, beef, eggs, salmon, tuna and dairy products like yoghurt and cheese that you can include in your rat's diet. Dairy products, however, should be given in moderation to your rat. You can also add some dog food as it is a good source of proteins.

Fresh fruits and vegetables
A major portion of your rat's diet should consist of vegetables and fruits. There are some fruits and vegetables that are beneficial to rats and some that are harmful. When you are giving your rat any fruit, make sure that the pit and the seeds are removed. Seeds such as apple seeds can be toxic. While the skin of most fruits can be given to rats, avocado seeds are known to cause a lot of health issues.

Some fruits and vegetables that you can include in the diet are:

- Apples
- Apricots
- Applesauce
- Bananas
- Avocados
- Beef
- Blackberries
- Blueberries
- Boysenberries
- Broccoli
- Cantaloupe
- Carrots
- Butternut squash
- Celery
- Cauliflower
- Cherries
- Choy
- Cold cuts
- Cooked sweet potato
- Cranberries
- Cucumber
- Green beans
- Grapes
- Green peppers
- Kale
- Honeydew melon
- Lettuce

- Kiwi
- Mashed potatoes
- Melons
- Papaya
- Peaches
- Pears
- Peas
- Plums
- Pomegranates
- Potatoes
- Pumpkins
- Raspberries
- Red peppers
- Strawberries
- Walnut
- Watermelon
- Yellow peppers

The fruits and vegetables that are harmful include:
- Dried corn
- Green potato
- Green bananas
- Mangoes
- Oranges
- Peanuts
- Poppy seeds
- Potato eyes
- Raw artichokes
- Raw beans
- Raw Brussels sprouts
- Spinach
- Raw onion
- Raw red cabbage
- Rhubarb

Foods that are hazardous to rats:
- Caffeinated drinks
- Chocolate
- Licorice
- Blue cheese dressing
- Candy

- Orange juice or any orange based foods
- Any junk food

Best treats for rats:
- Soya milk
- Fish sticks
- Dog treats
- Chicken bones
- Cooked rice and pasta
- Baby food
- Baby cereal
- Rice cakes
- Cheese

Always make sure that your rat has enough clean water along with fresh food. You can provide your rat with rodent chows such as lab blocks and milled pellets. A seed and nut based diet should be avoided as it makes your rat obese over time.

You will see several types of colorfully packaged supplements and rat foods that are available online. There are several options such as hay cubes, mineral pellets, vitamin pellets, seed mixes, chewable wood etc. that are usually chosen by pet owners. They make for good treats but are not recommended as primary diet. Pellet feed that has at least 16% protein is one of the options for a primary diet.

From time to time, you may also feel tempted to offer your rat table scraps. Make sure that you limit this to healthy foods like fruits and vegetables, lean proteins and whole wheat bread. This should be limited to 15% of your rat's diet. When you follow a healthy diet plan for your rat, you will not have to give them any supplements in the form of mineral or vitamin blocks.

When and how to offer foods
Rats are nocturnal creatures. They are active after sundown and should ideally be fed then. You will have to make sure that the rat is provided with a continuous supply of food. If the rat is storing several stashes of food around the cage, chances are that you are overfeeding him and have to cut back on the portions.

Any dry food can be given to the rat with the help of a food dispenser. Alternatively, a heavy ceramic bowl that will not tip over can be used. Dry and wet food should be offered in separate dishes so that you can clean out the fresh produce if you see any signs of spoiling

Tubes and other hiding areas in the cage can become contaminated with food debris. This should be checked everyday to make sure that you do not have issues like infections.

The amount of food that the rat consumes varies with age, breeding, health and the type of food that you offer. There are several factors like the time of the day and the temperature that will matter too. Usually rats eat more at night and will only nibble at food during the day.

4. Grooming the rat

Rats are very fastidious creatures. They spend close to 30% of their time awake cleaning and grooming themselves. Therefore, bathing them or shampooing them is not necessary.

One of the best ways to keep your rat clean is to brush him regularly. You can use a small toothbrush that is damp and just run it over the body to keep your rat clean.

However, rats will need a bath in case they have a case of the orange secretion due to excessive protein. They can also get into mud or debris while playing and get really dirty. This is when they will need a good bath.

Besides bathing your rat, trimming the nails and teeth is also extremely necessary to keep yourself safe and also the other cage mates of your rat safe.

Bathing the rat

To make bathing your rat simpler, it is a good idea to have a bathing kit in place. That way, you will have everything that you need in place to get your rat cleaned faster. Here are some things that you should include in your rat bathing kit:

- Nail clippers
- Mild shampoo
- A soft toothbrush
- Towels
- A blow drier that has a cool setting
- A bag of treats

Once the kit is ready, you can bathe your rat following these simple steps:
- Use the kitchen sink or the bathtub to bathe your rat. With the faucet, gently run some warm water on the body of the rat till the fur is wet. When wetting the head, make sure that you use a scoop of water in

your hands and gently run some water on the fur avoiding the hair, ears, eyes and nose.

- Place the rat on a towel and then lather with the mild shampoo. The shampoo should be kept away from the face.

- For rats that may have any scaly skin, particularly males that have been in a fight, you will have to comb the hair out with a toothbrush. The common areas of concern are the tail and the area behind the ears.

- The rat should be placed under running water to get the shampoo off completely. This process can be repeated if the soiled area is not fully clean.

- Once you have cleaned the rat fully, clean the toothbrush fully and comb the fur in the direction of growth. You should be very gentle when brushing the tail as it can get damaged quite easily. Always clean the tail from the base towards the tip and never the other way around.

- Take a dry towel and briskly wipe the body to get any excess water out.

- If the weather is warm, you can just let the rat dry in the sun. If not, you will need to use the blow drier to get your rat fully dry. When you do this, brush the coat and then dry with a cool setting. If you can place your rat on your lap while doing this, he will be a lot more comfortable.

- You must give your rat a treat after the bath so that he knows that it is a good thing.

Keeping the toenails trimmed
Sometimes, the nails of the rat can get too long. You will know this when they leave scratches in their play area or inside the cage. Frequent trimming is required to prevent the nail from getting caught and causing injuries. They can even cause wounds on the skin when they scratch or just play.

However, trimming the nails is no easy task. The feet of the rat are so small that spotting the quick can be hard. The quick is a vein that goes from the base of the nail to the tip. This is seen in all animals. If you cut the quick, it can lead to a lot of bleeding and can be traumatic to you and your pet.

In the initial period, you can take some assistance from your vet or from someone who has experience with rats. When you are ready to trim the nails yourself, you can do it at home with a few simple tools:

- Nail clippers
- A torch or other source of bright light
- Styptic powder
- Rat treats

It is possible to use the same clippers as humans as the rat's nails are tiny. Human nail clippers are easy to use and are also small enough. You can also find specific clippers for small animals in pet stores. You can choose as per your preference.

Hold a finger out horizontally and place the rat's feet at the edge. Then, you can examine each toenail to spot the quick. This can be hard to do in a room that is dimly lit. The area without the quick is lighter in color. Once you have spotted it, you can cut it slowly.

You can also ask someone to hold the foot of the rat while you look for the quick and cut the nails. If the nails are not too long, you can also use a nail file to get the job done easily. If the rat is squirming or moving too much, it is advised to just let the rat settle before you proceed to trim his nails.

That way, you will be able to avoid any accidents. In case you do clip the quick accidentally, you can apply some styptic powder to prevent any more bleeding. If you do not have access to styptic powder, you can also use corn flour to curb the bleeding.

In the beginning, take a few minutes to rest between the times you cut each toe nail. You can offer the rat a treat when you are done with each toenail. That way, they will get more comfortable with the process. As you gain more experience, you will be able to cut the nails of your rat very easily.

Trimming the teeth of your rat
Dental care is extremely important for rats. That will prevent any infections or diseases. You must also keep the teeth of the rat trimmed to prevent any injuries when he plays with you. Rats like to nip and lick as a sign of affection. If you do not trim the teeth, you can be seriously injured. In addition to that, trimming the teeth will also ensure that no damage is caused to your belongings in case the rat gets into any of your stuff.

With rats, brushing their teeth is not necessary. But, you will have to keep the teeth clean using other methods like providing the rat with chew toys, hard treats like dog biscuits, twigs of treats like peach, pear or apple. You can also give your rat wild grass to keep the teeth in good condition. Remember that rats have yellowish front teeth naturally. This should not be confused with the teeth being dirty.

It is also important to avoid foods like candy and chocolate that are high in sugar to keep the teeth of your rat healthy. You must also avoid sharing food as rats can obtain some bacteria through humans.

Overgrown teeth are the biggest problem with rats. They can be severely injured when they are eating as the large teeth can pierce through the gums of the animal. This is why trimming the teeth is one of the most important parts of oral hygiene in rats.

Make sure that you pay close attention to the alignment and growth of the teeth in your pet rat. The top and bottom teeth should be in line with each other. If you notice that they are uneven, crooked or overlapping, it is a sign of overgrowth of teeth.

You can trim the teeth of your rat at home. Since there are no nerve ends in the teeth, this process is painless for the rat. You can use dog or regular nail clippers to do the job. When doing this, make sure that you keep the length of both the incisors equal in length.

You can open the mouth of your pet rat using your finger. Then place the teeth that you want to trim against the finger and trim it slowly. It is recommended that you have the teeth clipped by the vet. While there is no pain there are chances that the teeth crack into the root when you clip them.

The vet can use a dental saw or burr to make a cut that is clean. You will also have to make sure that the teeth have been trimmed equally to prevent any discomfort to the rat. Uneven teeth can also cause wounds and abscesses in the mouth. There are several preventive measures like giving your rat good food, chew toys and also regular vet checkups.

When the rat has an issue of overgrown teeth, it is recommended that you have the teeth trimmed every three weeks for best results.

5. Cage maintenance

Keeping the cage of your rat clean is a very important step towards keeping him healthy. Several germs thrive in cages that are unkempt and can cause serious illnesses in rats.

While you can clean the cage thoroughly every fortnight or as required depending upon the number of rats you have in your home, you have to make sure that the food and water bowls are cleaned out everyday. Before you feed your rats, make sure that the food and water bowls are cleaned fully.

The bedding also needs to be changed more frequently depending upon how messy it gets. Cage maintenance requires a good schedule. Then, you can follow a few simple steps to keep your rat's habitat in great condition.

Tips to clean your rat's cage
Rats live in very close contact with the bedding and litter. Therefore, they must be kept very clean to prevent any accumulation of harmful toxins. You may have a litter box or some substrate lining the cage to collect all the waste and excreta. The bedding is the place where your rats rest. That is normally restricted to the nesting box.

To begin with, remove all the litter, toys, accessories and bedding material from the cage. Then you need remove any dust that is visible to you. This can be done by simply spraying the cage with water.

Use a brush or a scrub to get rid of any fussy debris. You can use any mild dishwashing soap to make it easier to clean the cage. A pressure nozzle is also good enough to get the rat's cage cleaned out and free from any debris.

All the accessories can be cleaned with a spray of water. Unless there is any feces or stubborn dirt on these accessories, they do not need to be scrubbed. For the smaller accessories, you can just soak them in the kitchen sink or in a small tub. Scrub them if needed and then proceed to disinfecting them.

Once the cage is fully free from all the visible dirt, move on to disinfect it thoroughly. This will take care of any microbes or pathogens lingering around in the cage. You can choose from an array of disinfectants. You can use products like Nolvasan, Oxyfresh, antibacterial liquid soap, Diluted bleach, vinegar and hydrogen peroxide. These disinfectants are mild and can take care of bacteria as well as viruses.

No matter what product you use, make sure you follow the instructions provided on the box. Spray the cage fully with the disinfectant and let it stay for the time period mentioned on the box. Each product needs different periods of time to get the job done. When using household products like vinegar or bleach, leaving them in for about half an hour should do the trick. In case there has been a viral outbreak among your rats, ask your vet for a recommended virucide.

Spray all the toys and accessories as well and let them soak in it for a while.

After the cage and the accessories have been soaked in for the given duration, you have to rinse them thoroughly. These disinfectants have several chemicals that may cause a lot of harm to the rat's health.

Use a power spray to rinse the cage and the accessories. Most disinfectants come with a very distinct odor. Make sure that the odor is gone fully before you dry the cage. Rinsing is the most important step in cleaning the cage to ensure that there is no chemical residue in the cage.

After rinsing the cage, you have the option of wiping everything dry. Air drying in the sun, however, is the better choice as the sunlight will kill most of the microorganisms that may have been left behind even after disinfecting the cage fully.

If there are any fabric accessories in the cage, they should be cleaned regularly. This includes hammocks, climbing ladders or just about anything that is made of cloth. These accessories should be cleaned at least once every week as they tend to get very dirty. This means that cleaning fabric accessories in between the schedule that you have set to clean the cage is very important.

All the fabric accessories should be washed with a hypo allergenic soap. You can either wash them by hand or just use the washing machine. If the cage has housed a rat that is unwell or might have been contaminated with parasites, you need to wash them with a small amount of bleaching powder and then soak them in hot water. When you use these disinfectants, it is mandatory to rinse the accessories thoroughly to get rid of any chemicals.

You can dry them all in the dryer of your washing machine or with simple hair dryer. These accessories become free from any infestations by parasites or other microorganisms when dried at high speeds for about 20 minutes. You also have the option of drying them in the sun.

Here are a few tips that you must keep in mind when cleaning the cage of your rat:

- Do not use any cleaner that has a perfume.

- Spot cleaning whenever you find too much litter or debris in the cage is required even in between the cage cleaning schedule.

- Make sure that your rat has some temporary housing when you are cleaning the cage.

- The accessories should be cleaned completely.

- The cage cleaning should be done in an area that is well ventilated and your rats must be kept away.

- Before you disinfect the cage, every bit of visible debris should be gone.

- If you are disinfecting a cage that has housed a sick rat, ask your vet to recommend a good disinfectant.

- The cage should be fully dry before the rats are placed back in.

- When possible, using the sun to dry the cage is highly recommended.

- Cages that are used as nursery cages should be cleaned out more often.

With these simple steps, you will have a cage that is spotless. Rats are extremely clean and therefore, need a clean cage in order to stay happy and of course, to be healthy.

6. Bonding with rats

Rats form very strong bonds with their owners. If you are willing to spend some time with your rat, you will realize that they are highly intelligent creatures who can be taught several tricks. Bonding with your rat takes some understanding of their general behavior and also learning how to handle them correctly takes time.

Once you have achieved that, you can use all the information to your advantage when you proceed to train your rat to perform various tricks.

Understanding rat behavior

Like any other animal, rats also have a certain body language that you can understand with time. It is true that every rat has a different personality. However, overall, they all display the same signs with their body language and learning this is a huge advantage for anyone who is new to the world of rats.

Wrestling and fighting

There is a big difference between fighting and wrestling when it comes to rats. They can have serious fights, especially when two aggressive males are housed together. When they fight, they can cause a lot of injury to one another. If you do not recognize a fight and stop them in time, you can have a rat with an amputated toe, ear or nail. When your rats are interacting with each other in a violent manner, watch for any signs of blood. If you notice this, then you can spray them with some water till they let go of one another to clean themselves.

One rat is clearly losing in the fight. You must grab this rat and move him to a separate box or cage. Once both the rats have settled down, you must treat any injury and then keep them in separate areas till they are properly introduced again.

On the other hand, wrestling is mostly play behavior as you will see in most animals. This is common in baby rats or kittens. There may be loud squeaking, mounting, pouncing and boxing where they stand on their hind legs and seem to be punching one another.

When they are doing this or just chasing one another, you do not have to be alarmed. In the case of the adolescent rats, this wrestling behavior is rougher. As they grow older, this behavior mellows down and the rats will spend a lot more time relaxing or sleeping. Their social activities are limited to grooming or just sniffing at each other. This behavior is also used as an outlet for hormones and also to settle dominance dispute. You can also wrestle with your rats when you play with them.

Mounting

This is a type of behavior that is mostly seen in adolescent rats of both genders. While most people consider this a sign of dominance, it has often been observed that mounting is not related to the status of the rat in the group. It is play behavior that also tends to be an outlet for hormones. Mounting behavior subsides quite easily in male rats. In case of the females, they will display mounting behavior for a longer time when they are in heat.

Teeth chattering and grinding

This behavior is also known as bruxing. It is a sign that your rat is calm and happy in most cases. It may also occur when the rat is frightened or sick. So, make sure you understand the context and associated body language. If the rat is bruxing after play, then it means that he is happy. However, if he is covering in one corner of the cage, you need to look for possible signs of illnesses or anything that may have scared him.

Licking

Most people believe that rats lick the fingers because of the salt content on them. This is, in fact, a social behavior displayed by rats. Rats tend to groom each other when forming bonds in a group. They will do the same to you when they begin to get comfortable and relaxed around you. In the case of older rats, licking is parenting behavior and also to assert dominance. The younger rats will lick as a sign of submission. You will see that during wrestling, the rat that has been pinned down will lick the one that is "winning". This is a sign that the game has come to an end.

When rats lick their owners, they are accepting them as the dominant one. It is also a sign of acceptance which shows that the rat knows that you do not mean any harm.

Bar chewing
This is a sign that the teeth of the rat are too long or that he is bored or nervous. This can be very annoying to the owners. It is seen mostly when rats live alone. It is possible to curb this behavior with a chew toys or by giving your rat a cage mate.

Interacting more with your rat also helps tremendously with this type of behavior. You can spend more time with the rat being outside the cage. Handling the rat regularly helps quite a bit. If your rat is in a new cage, wait for a few days and see if the behavior subsides. Sometimes, rats will use this behavior to communicate to you that the cage is too dirty or that they are hungry. Another simple way to reduce this behavior is to cover one part of the cage with a thick cloth. When rats have a solid wall and less light, they tend to be less nervous.

Head swaying
Vision is very different in rats when compared to other animals. They can see contrasting shades well and will also be able to see contours. However, they do not see depth or colors very well. When they are trying to visually recognize something, they will sway their head. This helps to move the object in their line of vision and makes them appear in front of the backdrop. This is seen when the rat is trying to judge a jump, when they see something that is interesting or something that is threatening. Rats that have lighter eyes such as beige rats or albinos have poorer vision and will display this behavior more. On the other hand, rats that are blind and those with dark eyes will not display this behavior.

Urinating
Usually rats will urinate when they are afraid. If you startle a rat by picking him up when he is still not ready, he will urinate on you. They will stop this behavior as they learn to trust you more. Urinating is also used to mark their territory. This is why rats will normally urinate on the arms or legs of the owner. If this is seen, you should discourage your rat from walking on surfaces that he urinates on or marks.

Biting
Among the rodents, rats are the least nippy ones. They will not simply bite you if you wake them up or startle them. They need to have a good reason to bite you. In addition to this, the bite of a rat is not as hard as a gerbil or a

hamster. There are some things that make rats bite. You need to assess this and do what it takes to curb that behavior.

First, rats bite out of fear. If they have been raised in an environment that is very stressful, they may bite as they as scared of people. They usually run away from people and will only bite when people are too persistent to handle them. They may even bite when they have been in a very bad fight or if they smell a lurking predator. If you handle your rat regularly, he is less likely to bite out of fear.

Rats are also scared of common human items like socks, Band-Aids or gloves. Normally, anything that covers the hands or the legs tends to make them fearful. You see, rats mostly recognize you by the texture of your body and smell. These things can confuse them and trigger an attack. It is best to avoid wearing them when you are around your rat. Even the gentlest of pets can bite when they are confused.

Second, rats sometimes bite by mistake. They may mistake your hand for a treat and land a bite if you have lotion or smell of food on your hand. Eventually rats learn to differentiate between treats and hands and will only lick your hand. They may sometimes miss the mark and bite your hand while trying to take a treat from them. It is best to offer larger treats to rats and to avoid giving them through the bars of the cage.

Third, rats like to tease people who are afraid of them. If you are afraid of rats, it is best to pet them when they are in the cage, through the bars. However, if you are hesitant or if you draw your fingers away suddenly, the rat will try to hold your hand in their mouth and pull you back. If you try to get away, they will clamp on harder. This is why you need to be extremely confident when handling your pet. Any hesitation will lead to nips or bites.

Fourth, a rat who is in extreme pain will bite you if you touch the area that is tender. In most cases, rats will squeak loudly or make a puffing sound before biting.

Fifth, aggression can lead to bites. This is normally seen in male rats. They will bite to assert dominance or will bite when you have handled another male rat. You can have your rat neutered to reduce aggression related bites.

Sixth, rats who have just had a litter or are pregnant will bite to defend themselves even from owners whom they are closely bonded with. If a female becomes nippy around her litter, know that she is just following her instinct. You should just let her be and not force any interaction till she is comfortable.

Seventh, nipping is a part of play. When you are wrestling with your rat or are playing with him, it is common for them to nip. These nips are generally very gentle and will not hurt you at all.

Taming your rat

Domesticated rats, as we have seen in the previous sections are very different from wild rats and are usually very social. They also tend not be nervous around people. These rats are usually accustomed to handling and are trusting towards human beings.

However, if you brought your rat home from a commercial rattery or from a pet store, the environment that they grew up in is extremely stressful. This makes them associate human hands with neglect and abuse as they might have been picked by the tail or picked up by people who are generally afraid of them. This makes them skittish around people and will also make them nippy.

In any case, a rat is shy when he comes to a new home regardless of his environment. It is very rare to see a rat who is brought from a good breeder with these issues as they are used to being handled very carefully and with a lot of affection.

The first thing that you need to know about rats is that they have the instincts of a prey animal. So expecting them to trust a large animal, including humans, in an instant is unreasonable. There are a few things that you can do to make your rat feel comfortable and less threatened in the initial period:

- Bring the rat home with a friend or sibling. Rats tend to feel safer in larger numbers. If you bring home more than one rat, they will be more confident when exploring their new space.

- Never force an interaction with your rat. Pulling your rat out of the cage, picking him up when he is evidently uncomfortable or cornering him in the cage to pet him will make him weary of you. Instead, wait for the rat to come to you. Just hold your hand inside the cage and the rat will come over and sniff your hand. You can place some treats on your palm and hold it out flat before the rat. Pet him gently and only until he is comfortable. You can later leave the cage open and hold your hand out outside the cage. If the rat is comfortable enough, he will approach your hand voluntarily.

- Using treats can be extremely helpful. They are the key to winning the trust of your pet rat. When your rat figures out that you are the source for yummy food and treats, he will begin to trust you quite a bit. You can pet the rat if he allows you while you are giving him a treat.

- Cats, dogs, ferrets and smaller animals should be kept away from the rat while you are taming him. Having a predator around will make the rat extremely uncomfortable and even nervous. They may become so agitated at times that they will nip you.

- Handle your rats in a dark area to begin with. Keep the lights dimmed when you play with the rat as they will be at ease. This is when most predators are asleep in the wild. So darkness is equivalent to safety in the case of rats.

- You must never startle your rat. In the wild, a predator will strike when the rat least expects it. This is why a sudden move or sound means an attack for any prey animal like the rat. They do not see very well and it is very important for you to approach them correctly. In an event that the rat nips at you, never scream or pull your hand away. While the rat is holding on to your hand or finger, just hold still and remain calm. When the rat calms down, he will let go on his own. That is when you can give him a treat to calm him down.

- When the rat is used to your hand and allows you to pet him without becoming nervous, you can begin to pick him up. Hold him under the belly or by the sides but never by the tail. Gently pick him up only when he is calm. When he lets you do this, make sure you spend as much time with your rat as possible. You can keep him on the couch with you, or just watch some TV with your furry friend. Eventually, the rat will be comfortable enough to perch on your shoulder while you attend to your chores. Keeping the cage in a room that you are often in will help. However, the room should not be very noisy and bright. Talk to your rat whenever you are near the cage. This helps build familiarity and the bond between you and your rat will improve with time.

Basic rat training
Rats are among the most intelligent rodents. They are also highly food motivated. This is a combination that allows you to train them quite easily. That said, it is very different to training a dog or a cat because rats are wired differently. They perceive things around them differently and will respond according to their perception.

When you are training your rat, negative reinforcement is completely out of the question. You must not scold or even flick the rat gently. This kind of training, although never recommended, is used with cats or dogs and does not cause a lot of issues. This is because in the wild cat and dog mothers will use growling or even a touch with the mouth as a method of disciplining.

This vocabulary is absent in case of rats. They are prey animals, which means that any sudden noise or unpleasant touch signals danger and makes them want to hide instinctively. If you resort to any form of negative reinforcement, your rat will only become more afraid of you. This will make them habitual of biting and running away from people.

There are some things that you can include in your basic training process with your rats:

Litterbox training: On their own, rats do not choose any random place to poop in. They will have a designated spot in the cage. Litterbox training is merely telling your rat that the spot that you choose is the best one. To litter train your rat, you need to really understand the natural behavior instead of trying to teach him new ones.

Rats will designate one or more corners as bathroom spots in the house. This area is opposite the feeding area generally. Sometimes, the litter box training turns the other way around and your rat will use it as an area to store leftovers or scraps and make it a garbage pile. Get a litter box that will fit into a corner and put where rats generally go. You should always place the litter box on the floor. If it is at a height, the rat will think that it is a resting spot.

If you see the rat sleeping in the litter box, you must add something more comfortable such as a soft bed or a hammock so it makes a more appealing resting spot. Then the litter box should be moved to another corner in the cage. Each day, pick up a few rat raisins and place them in this box and they will eventually learn that this is where they need to go and will also use it as a place to dispose any soiled bedding.

Teaching the rat to come: A rat will go anywhere where there is food. This is the basic rule that you can apply to your rat. To begin with, hold the treat out to your rat so he can see it. Then when you offer it to him say his name or any word that you want him to respond to. They will then learn that responding to their name will get them some food. You can then start to call their names out from a corner of the room. They are curious animals by nature and will respond to the sound or will come out to investigate. When they do that, give them a treat.

One very useful thing to do is to shake the box with the treats to make a rattling sound. This is a loud sound and will garner some response. This is very useful if your rat escapes from the cage and is lost.

Keeping them off limits: Rats are finicky creatures and will seldom go to any area that is sticky or unpleasant. So, placing some weak double sided tape around the area that you do not want them to enter makes them averse to it. You can alternatively get a bitter spray from any pet store and apply it on clothes or furniture to prevent your rats from chewing on it. Any loose wire in your house can be sprayed too.

Training them to find a safe house: There are several instances when the rat gets out of the cage and is unable to get home because they get scared or if they come back to the cage and find the door closed for some reason. This is why you need to designate some safe corners in the house that the rat can use so that he does not get lost trying to hide in a dark corner.

It is a good idea to use multiple nest boxes in the house. Then, you can keep changing the placement of these nesting boxes. The ones that the rats do not use can be placed in dark corners around your home. So, in case they are lost and are unable to get to the cage, they will approach the nesting box because of the familiar smell.

Remember that the nesting box should be easy for the rat to find but must be off limits to other pets. When you take the rat out to play, use the area around this nesting box so that they know where to find them. These boxes are extremely useful if you are taking your rat with you on a vacation. Then, they may be unable to find their way into the cage because of the unfamiliar territory. But having these nesting boxes around the room will reduce the stress that they experience.

Tricks you can teach rats
Rats are extremely intelligent and can be taught a host of different tricks. These tricks are mentally stimulating for the rat and can be a lot of fun for the owner. Some tricks that you can teach your rat are:

Standing up
This is an extremely simple trick that any rat will learn quite easily. If you are able to give your rat treats from your hand, then half the job is done.

Place your rat on a table top or a desk and make sure that there is nothing to distract him when you are training him. In case your rat is still not comfortable taking treats from your hand, then you can tie a piece of the treat to a stick or use a balled up piece of fabric with a small bell inside it.

70

Now, say the words "stand up" when you begin. The rat should be able to see the item in your hand when you give him the cue word. When he begins to investigate what is in your hand, just raise it above your rat's head till he follows it and is in an upright position. A clicker will help when he is in an upright position. Click and give him the ball or the treat.

If the rat is fussy and does not stand up immediately, raise the level as you go along. You can also move this on to simply sitting up. Then, you will wait say the word "sit" after he is upright and wait for him to settle on his hind legs. Give him the treat when he is in this position. Praising a rat when he does what you want will also work wonders.

Eventually, you will be able to get the rat to follow the item on his hind legs to make it look like he is walking upright. Make sure he is able to understand each step before you move on to the next one.

Sitting on your shoulder
You will love having your rat on your shoulder when you are just lounging in your house or going about your chores. They can be trained to sit on your shoulder for a long time. You can do this even more easily when the rat comes to you when you call his name and when he is comfortable being handled.

Let a friend set their hand on your shoulder while standing at arms-length. Then call the rat and say the word "shoulder". You must encourage your rat and coax him initially to get on the person's hand. Some may do it instantly. In some cases you will have to set the rat on the person's elbow and allow him to walk to your shoulder.

You can give him a treat when he gets to the shoulder in order to reinforce the behavior. In this case, praising works a lot better as the rat considers this a fun game.

When you are starting out, you can do so while sitting on a couch. This will make sure that the rat does not get hurt in case he gets spooked and decides to jump. Rats do not have very good perception of depth and will simply jump without thinking twice.

Then, you can teach the rat to walk up your hand to the shoulder when he is used to this trick. It will become a fun game for the rat and they will be more than happy to just jump up on your shoulder as it means that they get to spend more time with you.

Rolling a barrel

This is a slightly advanced trick that will require a great deal of patience on your part. You must teach the rat all the basic commands first. When he is confident with these tricks, it means that he trusts you enough to move to this step.

You will need a small barrel that is easily available in most pet stores. If you are unable to find one, you can also use a 6 inch piece of PVC pipe that you can decorate as you like. When you use a PVC pipe, add one layer of sandpaper over it to give your rat some traction. Place a carpet below the barrel to slow it down.

Set the barrel on two pieces of wood on either side to make a wall. This will help you even more. When your setup is ready, first set the rat on the barrel to get him used to it. If he jumps off, repeat it and praise him each time he decides to stay on the barrel longer. You can even hold him lightly on the barrel and praise him and offer a treat.

For the initial sessions, make sure that the barrel is steady and does not move. When the rat is very comfortable on the barrel, hold him lightly and move the barrel.

The next step is to wait for the rat to take a few steps as the barrel moves to find his balance. These sessions should be very short initially with the rat taking one or two steps. When he gets the idea of the barrel turning under his feet, he will hold his balance on it while taking a few steps. You need to give your rat a treat before he jumps off the barrel. If not, he will learn that jumping is the trick that you want him to perform. So, be patient. This can become a great trick if you decide to show your rat. It is also just a fun thing for the rat to do and for you to show off as a pet parent.

Rat bowling

Teaching a rat to push a ball towards ten small pins can be done in several ways. The first step is to set up an alley for the rat. This can be done with a few pieces of wood set to make a wall with one side open. Then, place a piece of smooth wood in the center on the floor. This alley can slant a little. The side boards will prevent the ball from going off track.

Set the rat sized bowling pins to resemble a bowling alley. You can buy these pins in a pet store or online. The best way to do this is to place a treat next to the bowling pin or rubbing some treat like yoghurt on the ball. Then give the command, "push" or "bowl" with the treat clearly visible to the rat. When the rat touches the ball, praise him well. It does not matter if the ball does not move. If the ball does move, you can place your rat closer to the ball and repeat the cue word.

Some rats will chase the ball down the alley. To stop this hold the rat while the ball rolls towards the pin. Eventually, they will just push the ball when they see it. It is a great mental activity for the rat and is a lot of fun for humans to watch, of course. However, it does require a lot of patience as the rat may not understand what you want from him in the first few sessions.

Going around
This trick is very easy for the rat to learn and you can teach just about any rat this trick. Place the rat on your shoulder. Then, hold your hands in front of you to make a circle with your arms. The circle should be right in front of your head.

Then, say the words "Go around". If you have someone assisting you, you can have them encourage the rat to walk on your arm with the help of a treat. They goal is to get your rat from one shoulder to the other after walking on your arms. When he does this correctly praise him generously and give him a treat.

The next thing you can do is to increase the circles. You can have someone stand with you and hold hands with them to make a bigger circle. So the rat will have to walk over your arms, and the other person's arms and shoulders to get to the other shoulder. This is a lot of fun for you and the rat.

When you are training your rat to perform tricks, patience is the key. You will have to keep a lot of treats handy to give them to your rat as he gets closer to completing the task. With rats, verbal praise goes a long way. So, do not forget to praise your rat for every small thing he achieves. You can pet him and use an excited voice to praise him.

The next thing you need to remember is that the training area should be free from any distractions. There should not be any toys or treats that your rat may find more interesting. Sound is also a major distraction for rats and they may even get frightened.

Lastly, be consistent. Set some time aside each day to train your rat to make sure that they learn the trick. Always proceed to a new trick when he has fully understood the previous one.

These tricks are very valuable in show rats. However, even when you do not intend to show your rat, teaching them tricks will help them stay healthy. Rats are extremely intelligent creatures that require a lot of mental stimulation to prevent unwanted behavior like bar chewing. This is also a great way to bond with your rat.

Dealing with bad behavior in rats

Poor nutrition, lack of exercise and improper handling can lead to behavioral issues in pet rats. In general, these creatures are extremely well behaved and are quite docile.

There are issues, however, with rats that have been rescued from abusive homes and in rats that are commercially bred without proper maintenance and hygiene.

If you notice any such bad behavior in your rats, there are a few measures that you can take to prevent and correct this behavior. Neglecting bad behavior in rats can lead to injuries to you and any cage mates that your rat has.

Dealing with an aggressive rat

Aggression is very noticeable in rats that are otherwise extremely docile. The traits of an aggressive rat include:

- Picking fights with cage mates regularly
- Biting and scratching when handled
- Biting and scratching when approached by his cage mates

What make a rat aggressive?

There are quite a few reasons why rats become aggressive. Some of them are:

- Hormonal changes. When rats are about 6 months old, the hormonal changes can be very overwhelming for them, making them aggressive.

- The rat is experiencing some form of stress. There are several stressors such as illnesses, change in the environment, death of a cage mate and sudden changes in temperature.

- The rat may be in pain. This makes him aggressive whenever he is handled.

- He has had unpleasant experiences in the past. The rat may have been abused by people, which makes him choose aggression as a defense mechanism.

- Territorial aggression is seen during the breeding season in rats. When any other rat of the same gender enters the marked territory, there may be several fights.

- Some rats are also genetically predisposed to being aggressive.

Aggression can be seen in male and female rats. Females tend to be aggressive when they have just given birth to a litter. This behavior usually subsides after she is done nursing the litter and when they leave the nest.

How to manage aggression?
Managing rat aggression is quite easy if you can give it some time and if you are consistent. There are some simple things that you can try to curb aggression in your pet rat.

Apply vanilla essence
Vanilla essence is one of the most useful things, especially when you are dealing with aggression related to territorial dominance. You can buy vanilla essence either online or in stores. Here is why vanilla essence works:
- Rats produce pheromones that gives them a unique natural scent. This can be offensive to another rat, making them want to fight the other rat off.

- Vanilla essence has a pleasant taste and smell which can curb aggression by covering the natural smell of the rats.

- Apply some vanilla essence on the back of the rat and at the base of the tail of the rats that are showing aggression towards one another.

- Sometimes, rats will also like the taste of vanilla essence and will try to lick it off, encouraging behavior that is very similar to grooming.

- This is very useful when you are introducing two rats but are having trouble making them get along.

- If your rat is aggressive towards you, rubbing some on your wrist will also help you. You can also rub some on your rat. That way, the scent on you and the rat is the same, making it less stressful for the rat to come to you.

Try to be very patient

Vanilla essence is only a temporary solution to aggression in your rat. In order to get to the root of the issue, you need to be very patient and learn about rat behavior in general. To do this you need to follow theses steps:

- If the aggression in your rat stems out of fear, the first thing you need to do is to gain your rat's trust. Learn to handle him correctly in order to do that.

- When you are dealing with any aggression between rats, using a plant mister can help. Spray some water on them when they begin to fight.

- You can also throw a towel on one of the rats to stop the fight.

Homeopathy
Unknown to most rat owners, homeopathy can work wonders when it comes to dealing with aggressive behavior in rats. The best part is that there are no harmful side effects.

- Ask your vet to recommend a homeopathic pet formula for aggression. One such options is PetAlive's formula for aggression.

- This formula is available in a granule form that can be dissolved in treats like yoghurt and offered to the rats.

- This formula is usually recommended for cats and dogs but it works well for rats as well.

- The effects are immediate and will calm your rat down in just a few days.

- The personality of the rat will not change when you do this. However, it will become easier to work with your rat's issues as you can let him out of the cage often and also handle him more.

- Socializing the rat with people and other rats becomes easier with these calming medicines.

Reduce stress

There are chances that your rat is just stressed and unwell which results in bad behavior. There are several things that you can do to reduce the stress and change his behavior for the better.

- Make a note of any changes in the rat's environment. Has he lost his cage mate? Have you changed the location of the cage? Or just about anything that is new to him can lead to stress. With some patience, this behavior can be eliminated.

- It might help to get your rat a cage mate if he is living alone. As long as the introductions are made correctly and the rats are getting along well, it will help the rat quite a bit.

- It is better to get a rat of the opposite gender. However, having them neutered and spayed before doing so will prevent any unexpected litters.

- If the aggressive behavior in your rat is sudden, then take him to the vet and have him checked up thoroughly to ensure that he is not suffering from any illness.

If your rat is still aggressive despite trying all these measures, then you can consider neutering him. Sometimes, hormones are the cause for all the behavioral issues in rats.

Rat rules you should know
In the animal world, there are some unsaid rules that you need to be aware of. Even with rats, there are a few rules that you need to abide by. If not, you put yourself at the risk of being bitten.

Rat rule No.1: If a finger or digit sticks in through the cage bars or if there is anything that is dangling through a cage wire, it will be nipped.

What you need to do:
- For the initial period, avoid sticking your finger into the cage. Even if it means offering food, do not hold it through the cage wire.

- When the rat is young, you can hold your finger in through the cage wire because they do not have any biting power at this point. They will nibble at your finger and will soon learn that it is not exactly tasty and it is better to just sniff around at the finger.

- This will make them tug at your finger in a friendly manner as they get used to it and will prevent any biting.

Rat Rule No.2: When food is held in through the cage wire, the rat will grab it as soon as possible before any other rat gets a hold of it. This is done even if the rat is all alone in the cage.

What you need to do:
- Make sure that the food pieces that you offer are long enough.

- When the rat is holding on to one end of the piece of food, hold the other hand up for them to smell.

- This will tell the rat where the food is coming from and will prevent them from biting the finger.

- Let the piece of food go only when the rat has had a good whiff of your hand.

- You will then hold out a piece of food for the next rat and repeat the same.

- This will also teach your rat that you will give every rat some food and that they need not fight for it.

- There will come a time when they will stop grabbing and yanking at the food. That is when you can hold out smaller pieces of food.

- Even if the food is close to your fingers, the rat will not mistake it for food and take a bite at your finger.

Rat rule No.3: When they are woken up from deep sleep suddenly, they will turn around and bite.

What you need to do:
- Approach the rat cautiously. Start by knocking on the cage door first. This will give the rat some time to prepare for the visitor.

- Never open the door and go straight in for the rat. They are never prepared and will instinctively bite.

- Remember that rats are prey animals and predators usually pounce with no warning. That is why they respond with self-defense.

Rat rule no.4: When rats are unsure, they bite as hard as possible.

What you need to do:

- Learn all about the body language of rats. That will help you distinguish between a rat who is afraid and a rat who is just cautious.

- Handle the rat regularly to make them trust you more.

- The rule with rats is that you never startle them. When you are approaching the cage, make sure that you make a lot of noise so that the rat is not caught off-guard.

- Rats have a very specific fear vocabulary. The sounds that they make are unique. They will change their breathing pattern and will have a certain stance. For instance, a rat who is backing away into a corner with the mouth open will bite when you approach him. You need to learn this well to avoid any aggression.

- Let the rat sniff you first and then you can pick him up and pet him.

The most important thing about rats is to make sure that they learn to trust you. This comes with cautious and correct handling. The next section will tell you all that you need to know about handling a rat.

Handling rats safely

When you are bonding with your rats, the most important thing is to make sure that you handle them correctly.

The first step is to get your rat to settle down in his new home as mentioned in the previous section. The rat should begin to trust you first. That can be accomplished by getting the rat used to your scent. Then, you can lure him towards you with treats. Once the rat knows that you are the source of food and treats, they will begin to come to you when you approach the cage. That is when you can begin to pick your rat up and get him used to being pet.

There are some tips that will come in handy when you begin this process with your pet rat:

- When you approach the rat, you need to make a lot of noise to let him know that you are there.

- Rats are easily coaxed to leave their hiding spots with treats. They love to munch on them, making it an extremely positive experience for them.

- If your rat seems unsure or nervous, you can use a spoon to offer these treats to them. The more they begin to trust you, the easier it will be to use your hand to provide these treats to them.

- When the rat leaves the hiding area, he will be curious about you and will slowly approach you.

- When the rat walks towards you, hold your hand out near the nose so that the rat can smell you.

- Rats use smell and taste to learn all about their environment. Make sure you keep your hand steady when they are still sniffing at it. Any sudden movement will make them nervous.

- While the rat is trying to get used to your scent, they may nibble at your knuckles or the fingers.

- When they do this, make a high pitched "eep" sound. This is the sound that rats use to tell each other that they are uncomfortable with what is happening around them.

- Once the rat is comfortable around your hands and fingers, you can begin to pet them.

- Rats are extremely social animals. They like the idea of physical contact as long as it does not cause them any stress.

- Rats love to be pet on their head and behind their ears. It is almost like you are giving them a massage.

- When you are petting your rat, be very gentle and slow. That will tell them that they need not be afraid of you as you will not hurt them.

Picking up your rat
Once your rat is comfortable around you, you can try to pick them up. In the beginning, this is met by some resistance from your rat. They are not exactly fond of being picked up.

The idea of being scooped up by someone who is much larger than them, makes the rat feel like they are under attack by a predator. In addition to that, when you hold your rat, they are several feet above the ground and will feel anxious. So, there are some tips that you can follow to make this easier for you and your rat:

- Let your rat get really tired. Rats usually sleep all day and will wake up around dusk. When they are beginning to wake up, you can approach them as they are less skittish and a lot easier to handle.

- You must not make any sudden movements in front of your rat. Make sure that you are slow and steady when you pick the rat up.

- Place your fingers under the rat's belly while you are petting the ears and the head. Rats are uncomfortable being touched on the belly but this is the best way to pick them up.

- Scooping the rat up with one hand under the belly will give you maximum stability. This is a central point that allows your rat to stay balanced while you are picking them up.

- You need to make sure that you have a good grip on your rat as they will be squirmy initially. They should not jump out of your hands.

- When you scoop your hand under your rat, let the tail rest on your arm. Placing your thumb on the lower jaw will prevent any bites.

- Once you have the right grip with one hand on the belly, cup the rat using your other hand. That will give you more security.

- Rats are extremely quick and will run and jump before you can realize it. This increases the chances of them falling and hurting themselves. Using two hands will prevent this.

- Take your rat around the house with you while you hold on to them with two hands. This makes you improve your relationship with your rat. Once the rat is comfortable, you can even let them crawl onto your shoulder and just hang around with you.

With these simple tips, you will be able to make your rat comfortable around you and will also be able to increase their sense of security around people   in   general.

Chapter 5: Breeding Rats

Rats become sexually mature when they are about 4-5 weeks old. This is when you should begin to house the rats separately if you do not have any accidental litters.

The average size of a litter is between 6 and 12 kittens. The gestation time ranges from 21 to 23 days. You will be able to detect pregnancy in a female rats at about two weeks. The abdomen will become rounder and the mammary glands or breasts begin to develop. When the female is pregnant, she will need ample bedding material to build her nest.

Females remain in heat all through the year and this makes it very easy for you to breed rats. There is no breeding season in particular with rats. However, when the temperatures are too low or high, breeding behavior will reduce. The heat in females occurs every 4-5 days and follows a regular schedule.

1. Responsible breeding

Before you make the decision of breeding rats, a few things need to be considered. Make sure that you never breed any rats that have had any infections in the mycoplasma. They should also be free from any respiratory diseases.

The litters are large and you may not have room for all the rats. So, you need to make sure that you have a plan in mind about finding them a good home. Never sell them to pet stores as they usually end up as reptile food. The goal of breeding pet rats should always be to produce kittens that are healthy and well socialized. Find adopters and breeders who can ensure this.

You must also consider the age of the rats when you decide to breed them. For females, the best time to breed them is when they are between 4-5 months old. It may be hazardous to their health if they are over 6 months of age when you breed them. The pelvic canal becomes narrower at this age making it hard to deliver the babies normally. You will have to opt for a caesarian delivery in this case to keep the rat alive.

In the case of males, age is not really an important issue. They are fertile even when they are old. If you want to breed a female for the second time, waiting for a couple of weeks after she has delivered the first litter is a necessary. The first litter must be weaned and she should have recovered physically and mentally.

2. Mating among rats

When you want to breed rats, all you have to do is place them in the same cage for about 10 months. They should be in sync with respect to the heat cycle. Initially, the female may resist the male being in the same cage. This behavior is reduced when she is in heat.

When the females come in heat, the vagina will open up. She will also show some behavioral signs. You can see this if you stroke her back when she is in heat. She will do a mating dance that involves darting forward, spinning around and then bracing the legs in a stiff position. Her head and tail will be lifted while the ears vibrate. This is a signal to the male that she is ready to mate.

The male will mount her as soon as she shows this behavior. He will start out by licking her and sniffing her. The scruff of the female is grabbed by the male during mounting. They will also mount many times when courting. This is mostly foreplay.

The male has to mount several times before he finishes the act. A single mounting, however, can get the female pregnant. This is why you should keep the male and female apart if you do not want a litter. Even when the female is not really in heat, the male can stimulate her to get to this state. You must also keep an eye on your rats as females may escape from the cage in pursuit of a male when she is in heat.

3. Preparing for birth

When you see the signs that the female is pregnant, you should make her comfortable to have a healthy litter. Her needs include good nutrition, exercise and a lot of nesting material. Before the litter is born, the male must be removed from the cage. There are chances that the male will hurt the kittens. In addition to that, the female will come into heat after giving birth in just 24 hours. This postpartum heat will lead to immediate pregnancy.

If the pregnant female has another female cage mate or a neutered male in her cage, they can be left together. For this, the cage should have ample space for the mother to have some privacy after giving birth. While rats are not known to hurt the kittens, they may steal them. This will lead to a tug of war leading to severe damage to the little ones.

A nursing female or a pregnant rat is extremely territorial and instinctive. That is why you must never put a new rat in the cage during this time as it leads to severe attacks.

Fostering is very easy with rats when they are nursing. They will even adopt babies from other species during this time.

You may notice a massive change in the personality of the rat when she is pregnant or nursing. This is because of the hormonal changes. You will see behavior like loss of interest in play or even aggression. Even the most submissive rat will become dominant after she gives birth. After they are done nursing, they will return to their normal behavior.

4. Birth of the baby rats

The entire process of birthing lasts for about two hours. A new kitten is born every 5-10 minutes. You will notice a bloody discharge from the mother's vagina. Then, as the contractions become bigger, the sides are sucked in entirely.

When the babies begin to arrive, the mother will sit up and deliver them using her teeth and hands. She will lick the newborns to clean the birth sac. The umbilical cord is usually eaten by the female along with the placenta.

If the baby is squeaking and wiggling, the mother accepts him in the nest. However, in case of a dead or weak kitten, the mother will not hesitate to eat him.

Female rats make great mothers. However, there may be some issues. In case the mother is too stressed from a long birth or has environmental stressors like loud noises or extreme pain during the delivery, she may kill even healthy babies and eat them. This can also occur when the diet of the mother is poor. If she displays this behavior, the babies should be removed from the cage and retuned when the mother is calm.

Once all the kittens are born, the mother will settle down and begin to nurse them. This is when there is no real danger of her harming or eating the kittens. If you wish to see the kittens, make sure you wait until the mother leaves the nest. You can handle the kittens but only after the mother has been removed from the cage. Contrary to popular myths, the mother will not abandon the litter if you leave your scent on them.

If the mother seems very nervous when you try to remove her from the cage, stop and try the next day. You will only force this separation if the babies have the umbilical cord entangled around their body. You must also examine the puppies regularly to rule out any health issues and to remove the ones that are dead.

In most cases, the birthing process is very smooth in rats. However, there may be issues, especially in first time mothers. When the mother begins the

84

birthing process, keep a close eye on her. If there are no signs of any kittens for two hours or more, then she may be having an obstructed birth.

Massaging the abdomen of the mother will help resolve this issue. If you see the baby stuck in the birth canal, you can lubricate the area and pull the rat out. Use forceps to get the baby out. After the first one is out, the rest will be born normally.

Sometimes, the mother may retain or reabsorb one of the fetuses. This is when you should ask your vet for antibiotics to make sure that there are no infections.

5. Caring for the kittens

When they are born, the kittens do not have any hair or teeth. The limbs and tails are very short and the kittens are deaf and blind. They will begin to develop hair after 7 days and will open their eyes after 14 days.

Keep an eye on the feeding process. Sometimes there may be one tiny rat who is unable to feed properly or is too weak to compete with the rest of the litter. When the babies are fed properly, you will be able to see the milk in the abdomen through the skin which is very thin. If one of them is not feeding properly, place some of the babies in a different cage. This will give the weak kitten a chance to suckle. Leaving a few of them in the cage will stimulate the production of milk. The mother will not pay attention if one of the babies is all alone with her.

As long as the babies are warm, you can keep them away from the mother for up to 4 hours. Place a heating pad below the container or place the cage near a light bulb. You can rotate the kittens every two hours to give all the weak kittens a chance to feed.

Baby rats will grow very fast. When they are about 2 weeks old, you need to make sure that you handle them as much as possible to make them more social. This is also the time when they begin to eat solid food. You do not have to worry about providing them with any food as the mother will share hers with them.

At the age of 4 weeks, baby rats usually begin to wean. After this age, it is alright to leave the females together. If the males are left in the cage, they may mate with their siblings.

It is very important to note that the wheel in the cage should be removed before the babies are born. If not, they can get trapped under it and suffocate.

If the mother dies during the birthing process, you can feed the babies with recommended baby formula. You will have to feed them every two hours for the first week and can increase the gap until they are two weeks old. Make sure that the kittens are warm. You can alternatively look for a nursing female to foster the litter.

Chapter 6: Health of your Pet Rat

The health of your pet rat is your biggest responsibility. You must make sure that your rat is in the best physical condition possible with good sanitation, good nutrition, proper quarantining and regular vet visits. While rats are quite hardy, there are some common health issues that you need to watch out for in your pet rat.

1. Signs of illnesses in rats

The first step to good healthcare is to be able to identify that your rat is unwell. Rats will show some clear signs when they are unwell. Here are ten signs that must look for in a sick rat:

- Porphyrin around the nose or eyes: This is usually a sign of respiratory diseases. You will see red discharge around the eyes or the nose of the rat.

- Piloerection: This is when the coat becomes very rough. This also indicates that the rat is nervous, stressed or cold besides being unwell.

- Lethargy: When a rat is unwell, he will show less interest in play and may refuse to leave the resting area.

- Licking: If your rat is licking one part of the body incessantly, it could imply that he has some pain in that area.

- Loss of appetite: As rats are food lovers, loss of appetite indicates that something is severely wrong. It indicates stomach issues or may also be the result of something being lodged in the throat.

- Cataracts: You will see a white, cloudy substance on the eyeball.

- Side sucking: The rat will suck in the sides of the abdomen to indicate issues like kidney stones.

- Staying in a corner: This is a definite sign of illness and could be pointing to serious health issues like cancer or strokes.

- Sudden weight loss: This can be an indication of general illness or some serious health conditions.

- Poor grooming: By nature, rats are extremely clean. If they are refusing to groom themselves, then it means that they are unwell.

When you see one or more of these symptoms, you need to see a vet immediately. While it could be a very simple issue such as indigestion, ignoring it can lead to complications and severe illnesses in your pet rats.

2. Finding a vet for your rat

Healthcare for any pet is incomplete without a good vet. You need to find a vet that specializes in caring for rats. There are a few simple tips that will help you find a vet who is experienced and also reliable:

- Make sure you look for a vet who encourages the idea of having a pet rat. There are several vets who lack respect for rats as pets and may suggest that you put them down instead of bearing the treatment costs.

- A vet who is great with cats and dogs may not have the knowledge that is required to provide right medical advice for your rat.

- Make sure that you look for a vet who is open to advice about rat health and is genuinely interested in treating your rat. You must begin to look for a vet for your rat from the time you decide to bring one home. That way, you will always be prepared for emergencies.

- Once you choose a veterinary clinic that matches your requirements, give them a call to understand their experience with rats. Ask to speak to the vet and make sure you have a few set of questions ready for him. You can for instance ask if a rat can be fed before surgery. A vet with experience will know that rats do not vomit and therefore, it is not really necessary to withhold food unless the type of surgery demands that you do.

- You must ask them how many rats are treated per day. They should have at least two rat patients each day, on an average.

- Also make sure that surgery success rate is at least 95%.

You must look for a vet who is closest to your home so that they are available in case of emergencies. You can check with local rat clubs, rat owners and even vets who treat other animals to find some leads. A vet who is available 24/7 or has an emergency care process is recommended.

Taking your rats to the vet

Visiting a vet can be very stressful to your rat. This is because of the different scents of other animals around the clinic. Most of these scents are those of predators, making rats even more uncomfortable. It is up to you to keep your rat calm every time you take him to the vet. You can do this with a few simple tips.

- Get a separate cage for your rat to take them to the vet. This cage should be smaller and you should be able to see your rat at all times.

- You have the option of a small cat carrier or even a plastic tub that has a fews hole poked in the top. The box is not the best idea as the rat cannot see you. Your presence will give your rat a lot of comfort.

- Place several blankets inside the cage. Fleece blankets or towels work best. This will give a rat who is skittish some option to hide in or dig into. They may hide in the blanket and will pop their head out from time to time to make sure that you are around.

- Taking a friend along for your rat can make them feel very comfortable. If your rat has a cage mate that he bonds with very well, taking him along will keep your rat more comfortable and less stressed.

- Take some treats along with you. This can prevent the rat from running away from the vet table. While the rat enjoys the treat you can have the vet examine him.

- Hold your rat firm when the vet is examining him. They may not like being handled by the vet and it is best that you hold them and listen to the directions given to you by your vet for a successful examination.

When the rat is sick or injured, making sure that they are calm even before they go to the vet is mandatory. You can place the rat in a quiet and warm place in your home till they are relaxed and then take him to the vet.

3. Common health issues in rats

Like all species of animals, there are some health issues that are common in case of rats. These illnesses are classified as below:

Respiratory diseases

Respiratory conditions that are caused by infectious agents are most common in rats. There are three main pathogens involved, namely:

- *Mycoplasma pulmonis*

- *Streptococcus pneumoniae*
- *Corynebacteriumkutscheri*

There are two common respiratory diseases that are seen in rats:

Chronic Respiratory Disease
Also known as murine respiratory mycoplasmosis, this condition reduces the lifespan of rats. It is caused by *Mycoplasma pulmonis.* The common clinical signs are:
- Nasal discharge
- Snuffling
- Polypnea
- Labored breathing
- Ruffled coat
- Hunched posture
- Red tears
- Weight loss
- Tiled head

Treatment
- Administration of doxycycline and enrofloxacin for 14 days can reduce symptoms.
- Nebulization therapy
- Providing bronchodilators to improve breathing
- Removing bedding regularly and replacing it clean one to reduce ammonia fumes in the cage.

Bacterial pneumonia
This condition is almost always caused by *Streptococcus pneumonia.* It is more common in the younger rats when compared to the older ones. The clinical symptoms include:
- Abdominal breathing
- Labored breathing
- Snuffling

Treatment
- Oral medications such as cloaxcillin or amoxicillin.

Viral infections
This is very common in rats, especially when they are not maintained well and when the cage conditions are poor.

The most common infection is by a strain of virus that is called the Sialodacryoadentitis virus. This is a virus that leads to inflammation.

In rats with this condition, the salivary glands and the lacrimal glands become swollen. So the rat appears like it has mumps. In severe cases, it may become necessary to surgically remove the swollen glands as they cannot be treated with any medication.

Rats may develop ocular lesions when they are affected by this virus. There are several types of lesions such as:
- Kertitis
- Corneal ulcers
- Hyphema
- Synechia
- Conjunctivitis

Parasitic infections
There are several parasites that rats are hosts for. These parasites can be internal or external and cause several health issues. The common parasites found in rats are:

Mites

There are various types of mites that are found in pet rats:

Rat fur mites

These are the most common types of mites found in rats. They cause a lot of itching and are very hard to find. In case of any rat fur mite possibility, a vet will recommend treatment whether they have been found on the body or not.

Ear mange mites

These mites only live on rats. An infection leads to the following symptoms:

- Crusty ears
- Scabs on the tail, nose, ears and feet

Tropical rat mites
These are the least common type of mites that are visible to the human eye when they have sucked blood. They can also bite human beings.
Treatment for mite infections
- Topical medication such as Revolution
- Application of Vaseline or diatomaceous earth on scabby areas

Worms orhelminths

These parasites live in the digestive tract of the rat and are associated with poor hygiene. They can also be carried by other pets like cats. Common signs of infection are:

- Diarrhea
- Loss of appetite
- Sudden weight loss
- Chewing and licking of rectal areas
- Worms in feces
- Severe infection causes intestinal blockage or perforation
- Liver enlargement in case of tape worms

Treatment

- Anti-parasitic medication
- Sanitization of the rat's immediate environment

Other health issues in rats

There are several other health disorders that mainly affect rats such as:

Ear infections:

The common symptoms are:

- Head tilting
- Lethargy
- Lack of balance

Treatment

- Steroid injections
- Antibiotics
- The rat should be taken to a vet before giving him any medication as these symptoms are seen in several other conditions.

Bumblefoot

This is seen very commonly in rats. It is mostly the result of any injury to the foot. A small cut or scrape that gets infected leads to bumblefoot. The symptoms are:

- Calluses that grow in size
- Scabs that open and bleed
- Abscesses
- Chronic inflammation

Treatment

- Disinfecting and cleaning the wound properly

- A small round of antibiotics
- Cleaning the cage to check for sharp objects

Benign growths

In rats, tumorous growths are common. They could just be benign growths and are not necessarily cancerous. These lumps are very common in the case of females and are seen in the mammary glands.

If the vet assures you that the tumor is benign, you need not opt for surgery unless it is causing mobility or other issues. In the case of rats, the anesthesia used during surgery is more dangerous than the disease itself. In addition to that, the stress of surgery may also kill the rat.

When a benign tumor is successfully removed with surgery, it almost never comes back again. But the benign growth can come back in a different part of the body.

Abscesses

Abscesses can be very hard for you and your rat. They are usually caused by an infection. If there is more than one rat in your home, make sure that they are separated in case of any abscesses.

The signs are:

- Painful lumps
- Puss in case the lump breaks

Treatment
- Clean the area with warm salt water
- Antibiotics can be provided to prevent any further infections.

Tumors

Rats will develop malignant tumors just as easily as they develop benign ones. These tumors will be back even after surgery. If you suspect a malignant tumor in your rat, make sure you talk to your vet.

The decision of whether you want to opt for surgery or put the rat down should be made in a week of the diagnosis of the tumor.

Prevention is the only cure with cancerous growths in rats. Providing them with a good diet will help curb the chances of malignant tumors.

Strokes

This is a common condition in old rats. If they are obese or have had a history of several illnesses at a young age, they are more prone to strokes at an older age.

The symptoms are very similar to that of an ear infection. They can cause varying levels of infections and you need to assess how bad the stroke is before you decide upon the treatment process.

Rats should be kept very healthy at all times. This is because there are chances of contracting zootonic diseases from them. These are diseases that affect both humans and rats. Conditions like rat bite fever or parasitic dermatitis can be contracted through rats.

First aid for rats
Having a rat at home means that you need to be prepared for emergencies. You never known when a rat may have a fall or a crash that could lead to serious injuries. Knowing basic first aid can save your rat's life.

Preparing a first aid kit

You need to have all the supplies that you may need in case of an emergency. The first aid kit for your rat should consist of the following:

- Cotton wool pads
- Sharp scissors
- Cotton buds
- Nail clippers
- Tweezers
- 1,2 and 5 ml syringes to administer oral medicine and to wash wounds
- Cohesive bandage
- Sterile saline eye drops
- Styptic powder
- Haemostatic plaster
- Sterile salt solution
- Antiseptic cleaning lotion

Dealing with common injuries
- **Crush injuries:** These occur when the rat gets trapped under or in between things. Check for visible damage. These injuries are usually internal so avoid handling the rat too much and make sure you call your vet.

- **Degloved tail:** Always have some painkillers handy as this condition can occur at anytime. It leads to severe bleeding and should be left untouched till you can see the vet. The tail will fall off eventually with proper administration of antibiotics and painkillers.

- **Trapped toes and feet:** In the case of excessive bleeding, apply some styptic powder to reduce it. There are usually just minor bruises. In case the bleeding does not stop and there are signs of immobility due to broken bones, do not handle the rat too much and get him to the vet immediately. Restrict climbing and administer recommended painkillers to reduce inflammation and pain.

- **Falls:** Falls can lead to several injuries from ruptured liver to spine injuries. Most of these injuries are internal. If the rat just shakes off and moves away, keep him under observation for a while. He should be shifted to a warm and quiet place to recover from the shock. Avoid handling the rat when he is under observation. Any abnormality requires immediate veterinary attention.

- **Scalds:** There may be time when your rat decides to investigate a hot drink or stove. If there are any scalds, they should be rinsed under cold water immediately. He should be allowed to recover from shock in a quiet, warm room.

- **Poisoning:** The biggest issue with rats is that they do not have the ability to vomit. This puts them at a high risk of poisoning. Make sure that your rat is in a quiet room and contact your vet immediately. If the poisoning is mild, it can be diluted with a lot of fluids. In some cases, antidotes are provided. If the rat refuses to drink fluids, they will be administered intravenously.

- **Electrocution:** Prevention is the only cure with electrocution by keeping all electric cords out of bounds. In case of an accident, check for a heartbeat. If the heart is beating but the rat is not breathing, place your mouth over his nose and mouth and breathe out some air. In case the heartbeat stops, the rat should be placed on a hard surface and a few sharp taps should be delivered on the chest. The rate of success is not high in these cases but you should try nevertheless.

Make sure your rat has a separate carrier to take him to the vet or to separate him from a group if you have multiple rats at home. Also, keep your vet's number handy at all times and make sure it is available to anyone who is taking care of your rat while you are away.

Chapter 7: Cost of Owning a Rat

Rats are certainly among the least expensive pets. However, there are some expenses that you should be willing to set aside a budget for. Rats usually live for about 3 years and you should be able to take care of these expenses for that period:

- Cost of the rat: $10-$20 or £5-£15 depending on the breed.
- Rat food: $3-6 or £2-£4 per month
- Cage: $30-$100 or £15-75 depending on size and build material
- Toys: $2-$7 or £1-£5 per toy
- Bedding: $7-$10 or £5-£7 per month
- Veterinary care: $35-$50 or £20-£40 per visit
- Spaying and neutering: $50-$100 or £35-£70
- Surgeries: $35-$100 or £15-£75 depending upon the complexity of the surgery.

There may be miscellaneous expenses including fresh produce. You need to set aside an additional $20 or £15 per month for any unexpected expense.

Conclusion

Thank you for choosing this book. Hopefully you have an insight into the world of rat parents. The book states all the responsibilities that you will have as a rat owner and you must only bring one into your home when you are completely ready.

Besides the owner of the rat, the entire family should be well informed about the rat. So make sure that they have all the important information available to them. That way, you can have someone reliable to care for your rat in case you are not available.

The more you learn about rats and their requirements, the better the care that you will be able to provide. Here's to hoping that you have a wonderful relationship with your little furry buddy.

References

Collecting as much information about rat care is the best way to keep them healthy and happy. The Internet is one of the best sources of information. Additionally, you can join a rat club or subscribe to their newsletters. It also helps to talk to a couple of rat parents or to seek advice from the vet or the breeder that you purchased your rat from.

Here are some websites that will be able to provide you with valuable information with respect to good rat care:

- www.aboutpetrats.com
- www.ratcentral.com
- www.neratsociety.co.uk
- www.peteducation.com
- www.80stoysale.com
- www.ratguide.com
- www.members.madasafish.com
- www.pets4homes.co.uk
- www.theagilerat.com
- www.ratchatter.com
- www.ratfanclub.org
- www.afrma.org
- www.petcha.com
- www.animals.mom.me
- www.ratsforpets.blogspot.in
- www.hoaxes.org
- www.rattitude.com
- www.humanesociety.org
- www.thespruce.com
- www.rspca.org.uk
- www.kb.rspca.org.au
- www.pethelpful.com
- www.peteducation.com
- www.drsfostersmith.com
- www.jollyes.co.uk
- www.curiousv.com
- www.understandingpetfancyrats.com
- www.sciencing.com
- www.allourpaws.com
- www.lovethatpet.com
- www.smallangelsrescue.org

- www.ratsauce.com
- www.shadowrat.com
- www.nfrs.org
- www.northstarrescue.org
- www.pets.costhelper.com
- www.pets4homes.co.uk
- www.petmd.com
- www.msdvetmanual.com
- www.exoticpetvet.net